The New York Idea

by Langdon Mitchell

Single copies of plays are sold for reading purposes only. The copying or duplicating of a play, or any part of play, by hand or by any other process, is an infringement of the copyright. Such infringement will be vigorously prosecuted.

Baker's Plays
7611 Sunset Blvd.
Los Angeles, CA 90042
bakersplays.com

NOTICE

This book is offered for sale at the price quoted only on the understanding that, if any additional copies of the whole or any part are necessary for its production, such additional copies will be purchased. The attention of all purchasers is directed to the following: this work is fully protected under the copyright laws of the United States of America, the British Commonwealth, including Canada, and all other countries of the Copyright Union. Violations of the Copyright Law are punishable by fine or imprisonment, or both. The copying or duplication of this work or any part of this work, by hand or by any process, is an infringement of the copyright and will be vigorously prosecuted.

This play may not be produced by amateurs or professionals for public or private performance without first submitting application for performing rights. Licensing fees are due on all performances whether for charity or gain, or whether admission is charged or not. Since performance of this play without the payment of the licensing fee renders anybody participating liable to severe penalties imposed by the law, anybody acting in this play should be sure, before doing so, that the licensing fee has been paid. Professional rights, reading rights, radio broadcasting, television and all mechanical rights, etc. are strictly reserved. Application for performing rights should be made directly to BAKER'S PLAYS.

No one shall commit or authorize any act or omission by which the copyright of, or the right to copyright, this play may be impaired. No one shall make any changes in this play for the purpose of production.

Publication of this play does not imply availability for performance. Both amateurs and professionals considering a production are strongly advised in their own interest to apply to Baker's Plays for written permission before starting rehearsals, advertising, or booking a theatre.

Whenever the play is produced, the author's name must be carried in all publicity, advertising and programs. Also, the following notice must appear on all printed programs, "Produced by special arrangement with Baker's Plays."

Licensing fees for THE NEW YORK IDEA are based on a per performance rate and payable one week in advance of the production.

Please consult the Baker's Plays website at www.bakersplays.com or our current print catalogue for up to date licensing fee information.

Copyright © 1907 by Harrison Grey Fiske

(Copyright assigned by Harrison Grey Fiske to Langdon Mitchell, January, 1908)

Copyright © 1908 by Langdon Mitchell

Copyright © 1936 (In Renewal) by Marion Lea Mitchell

Made in U.S.A.
All rights reserved.

THE NEW YORK IDEA
ISBN **978-0-87440-743-3**
#1168-B

THE PEOPLE

PHILIP PHILLIMORE, *a Judge on the bench, age 50.*

GRACE PHILLIMORE, *his sister, age 20.*

MRS. PHILLIMORE, *his mother, age 70.*

MISS HENEAGE, *his aunt, age 60.*

MATTHEW PHILLIMORE, *his brother—a bishop, age 45.*

WILLIAM SUDLEY, *his cousin, age 50.*

MRS. VIDA PHILLIMORE, *his divorced wife, age 35.*

SIR WILFRID CATES-DARBY.

JOHN KARSLAKE, *lawyer, politician and racing-man, age 35.*

MRS. CYNTHIA KARSLAKE, *his divorced wife, age 25.*

BROOKS, *Mrs. Phillimore's footman.*

TIM FIDDLER, *Mr. Karslake's trainer.*

NOGAM, *his valet.*

THOMAS, *the family servant of the Phillimores, age 45.*

BENSON, *Mrs. Vida Phillimore's maid, age 20.*

Copy of the Program of the First Production

LYRIC THEATRE

WEEK BEGINNING MONDAY EVENING,
NOVEMBER 19, 1906.
Matinee Saturday.

Under the Direction of HARRISON GREY FISKE

Mrs. Fiske

—AND—

The Manhattan Company

Presenting a Play in Four Acts, Entitled

THE NEW YORK IDEA

By Langdon Mitchell

THE PEOPLE OF THE PLAY

PHILIP PHILLIMORE .... *Charles Harbury*

MRS. PHILLIMORE, his mother .... *Ida Vernon*

THE REVEREND MATTHEW PHILLIMORE, his
 brother .... *Dudley Clinton*

GRACE PHILLIMORE, his sister .... *Emily Stevens*

MISS HENEAGE, his aunt .... *Blanche Weaver*

WILLIAM SUDLEY, his cousin .... *William B. Mack*

MRS. VIDA PHILLIMORE, his divorced wife .. *Marion Lea*

BROOKS, her footman .... *George Harcourt*

BENSON, her maid .... *Belle Bohn*

SIR WILFRID CATES-DARBY .... *George Arliss*

JOHN KARSLAKE .... *John Mason*

MRS. CYNTHIA KARSLAKE, his divorced
    wife .... *Mrs. Fiske*

NOGAM, his valet .... *Dudley Digges*

TIM FIDDLER .... *Robert V. Ferguson*

THOMAS, the Phillimores' family servant .... *Richard Clarke*

ACT I—Drawing-Room in the Phillimore house, Washington Square.
Wednesday afternoon, at five o'clock.

ACT II—Mrs. Vida Phillimore's Boudoir, Fifth Avenue.
Thursday morning, at eleven.

ACT III—Same as Act I.
Thursday evening, at ten.

ACT IV—John Karslake's House, Madison Avenue.
Thursday, at midnight.
Scene—New York.   Time—The Present

The production staged by Mr. and Mrs. Fiske.

To Marion Lea

The New York Idea

ACT ONE

SCENE: *Living room in the house of* PHILIP PHILLIMORE. *Five* P. M. *of an afternoon of May. The general air and appearance of the room is that of an old-fashioned, decorous, comfortable interior. There are no electric lights and no electric bells. Two bell ropes as in old-fashioned houses. The room is in dark tones inclining to sombre and of old-fashioned elegance.*

AT RISE: *Discovered* MISS HENEAGE, MRS. PHILLIMORE *and* THOMAS. MISS HENEAGE *is a solidly built, narrow minded woman in her sixties. She makes no effort to look younger than she is, and is expensively but quietly dressed, with heavy elegance. She commands her household and her family connection, and on the strength of a large and steady income feels that her opinion has its value.* MRS. PHILLIMORE *is a semi-professional invalid, refined and unintelligent. Her movements are weak and fatigued. Her voice is habitually plaintive and she is entirely a lady without a trace of being a woman of fashion.* THOMAS *is an easy-mannered, but entirely respectful family servant, un-English both in style and appearance. He has no deportment worthy of being so called, and takes an evident interest in the affairs of the family he serves.* MISS HENEAGE, *seated at the tea-table, faces footlights.* MRS. PHILLIMORE, *seated left of table.* THOMAS *stands near by. Tea things on table. Decanter of sherry in coaster. Bread and butter on plate. Vase with flowers. Silver match-box. Large old-fashioned tea urn. Guard for flame. "Evening Post" on tea-table.* MISS HENEAGE *and* MRS. PHILLIMORE *both have cups of tea.* MISS HENEAGE *sits up very straight, and pours tea for* GRACE, *who enters from door* L. *She is a pretty and fashionably dressed girl of twenty. She speaks superciliously, coolly, and not too fast. She sits on the sofa,* L., *and does not lounge. She wears a gown suitable for spring visiting, hat, parasol, gloves, etc.*

GRACE. (*Crosses and sits.*) I never in my life walked so far and found so few people at home. (*Pauses. Takes off gloves. Somewhat querulously.*) The fact is the nineteenth of May is ridiculously late to be in town. (*Pause.* THOMAS *comes down* L. *table.*)

MISS HENEAGE. Thomas, Mr. Phillimore's sherry?

THOMAS. The sherry, ma'am. (THOMAS *nods and indicates table up* L.)

MISS HENEAGE. Mr. Phillimore's *Post?*

THOMAS. (*Same business. Pointing to "Evening Post" on tea-table.*) The *Post*, ma'am.

MISS HENEAGE. (*Indicates cup.*) Miss Phillimore.

(THOMAS *takes cup of tea to* GRACE. *Silence. They all sip tea.* THOMAS *goes back, fills sherry glass, remaining round and about the tea-table. They all drink tea during the following scene.*)

GRACE. The Dudleys were at home. They wished to know when my brother Philip was to be married, and where and how?

Miss Heneage. If the Dudleys were persons of breeding, they'd not intrude their curiosity upon you.

Grace. I like Lena Dudley.

Mrs. Phillimore. (*Speaks slowly and gently.*) Do I know Miss Dudley?

Grace. She knows Philip. She expects an announcement of the wedding.

Mrs. Phillimore. I trust you told her that my son, my sister and myself are all of the opinion that those who have been divorced should remarry with modesty and without parade.

Grace. I told the Dudleys Philip's wedding was here, tomorrow.

(Thomas *at back of table ready to be of use.*)

Miss Heneage. (*To* Mrs. Phillimore, *picking up a sheet of paper which has lain on the table.*) I have spent the afternoon, Mary, in arranging and listing the wedding gifts, and in writing out the announcements of the wedding. I think I have attained a proper form of announcement. (*She takes the sheet of note paper and gives it to* Thomas.) Of course the announcement Philip himself made was quite out of the question. (Grace *smiles.*) However, there is mine. (*Points to paper.* Thomas *gives list to* Mrs. Phillimore *and moves up stage.*)

Grace. I hope you'll send an announcement to the Dudleys.

Mrs. Phillimore. (*Reads plaintively, ready to make the best of things.*) "Mr. Philip Phillimore and Mrs. Cynthia Dean Karslake announce their marriage, May twentieth, at three o'clock, Nineteen A, Washington Square, New York." (*Replaces paper on* Thomas's *salver.*) It sounds very nice. (Thomas *hands paper to* Miss Heneage.)

Miss Heneage. (Thomas *up stage.*) In my opinion it barely escapes sounding nasty. However, it is correct. The only remaining question is—to whom the announcement should not be sent. (*Exit* Thomas.) I consider an announcement of the wedding of two divorced persons to be in the nature of an intimate communication. It not only announces the wedding—it also announces the divorce. (*She returns to her teacup.*) The person I shall ask counsel of is cousin William Sudley. He promised to drop in this afternoon.

Grace. Oh! We shall hear all about Cairo.

Mrs. Phillimore. William is judicious.

(*Reënter* Thomas.)

Miss Heneage. (*With finality.*) Cousin William will disapprove of the match unless a winter in Cairo has altered his moral tone.

Thomas. (*Announces.*) Mr. Sudley.

(*Enter* William Sudley, *a little oldish gentleman. He is and appears thoroughly insignificant. But his opinion of the place he occupies in the world is enormous. His manners, voice, presence are all those of a man of breeding and self-importance.*)

Mrs. Phillimore *and* Miss Heneage. (*Rise and greet* Sudley; *a little tremulously.*) My dear William!

(*Exit* Thomas.)

Sudley. (*Shakes hands with* Mrs. Phillimore, *soberly glad to see them.*) How d'ye do, Mary? (*Same business with* Miss Heneage.) A very warm May you're having, Sarah.

Grace. (*Comes to him.*) Dear Cousin William!

Miss Heneage. Wasn't it warm in Cairo when you

left? (*She will have the strict truth, or nothing; still, on account of* Sudley's *impeccable respectability, she treats him with more than usual leniency.*)

Sudley. (*Sits* L.) We left Cairo six weeks ago, Grace, so I've had no news since you wrote in February that Philip was engaged. (*Pause.*) I need not to say I consider Philip's engagement excessively regrettable. He is a judge upon the Supreme Court bench with a divorced wife—and such a divorced wife!

Grace. Oh, but Philip has succeeded in keeping everything as quiet as possible.

Sudley. (*Acidly.*) No, my dear! He has not succeeded in keeping his former wife as quiet as possible. We had not been in Cairo a week when who should turn up but Vida Phillimore. She went everywhere and did everything no woman should!

Grace. (*Unfeignedly interested.*) Oh, what did she do?

Sudley. She "did" Cleopatra at the tableaux at Lord Errington's! She "did" Cleopatra, and she did it robed only in some diaphanous material of a nature so transparent that—in fact she appeared to be draped in moonshine. (Miss Heneage *indicates the presence of* Grace. *Rises; to* c.) That was only the beginning. As soon as she heard of Philip's engagement, she gave a dinner in honor of it! Only divorcées were asked! And she had a dummy—yes, my dear, a dummy—at the head of the table. He stood for Philip—that is he sat for Philip! (*Rises, and goes up to table.*)

Miss Heneage. (*Irritated and disgusted.*) Ah!

Mrs. Phillimore. (*With dismay and pain.*) Dear me!

Miss Heneage. (*Confident of the value of her opinion.*) I disapprove of Mrs. Phillimore.

Sudley. (*Takes cigarette.*) Of course you do, but has Philip taken to Egyptian cigarettes in order to celebrate my winter at Cairo? (*Comes below chair.*)

GRACE. Those are Cynthia's.

SUDLEY. (*Thinking that no one is worth knowing whom he does not know.*) Who is "Cynthia"?

GRACE. Mrs. Karslake—She's staying here, Cousin William. She'll be down in a minute.

SUDLEY. (*Shocked.*) You don't mean to tell me—?—! (*To armchair, L.*)

MISS HENEAGE. Yes, William, Cynthia is Mrs. Karslake—Mrs. Karslake has no New York house. I disliked the publicity of a hotel in the circumstances, and accordingly when she became engaged to Philip, I invited her here.

SUDLEY. (*Suspicious and distrustful.*) And may I ask who Mrs. Karslake is?

MISS HENEAGE. (*With confidence.*) She was a Deane.

SUDLEY. (*Crosses up back of table R., sorry to be obliged to concede good birth to any but his own blood.*) Oh, oh—well the Deanes are extremely nice people. (*Goes to table.*) Was her father J. William Deane?

MISS HENEAGE. (*Still more secure; nods.*) Yes.

SUDLEY. (*Giving in with difficulty.*) The family is an old one. J. William Deane's daughter? Surely he left a very considerable—

MISS HENEAGE. Oh, fifteen or twenty millions.

SUDLEY. (*Determined not to be dazzled.*) If I remember rightly she was brought up abroad.

MISS HENEAGE. In France and England—and I fancy brought up with a very gay set in very gay places. In fact she is what is called a "sporty" woman.

SUDLEY. (*Always ready to think the worst.*) We might put up with that. But you don't mean to tell me Philip has the—the—the—assurance to marry a woman who has been divorced by—

MISS HENEAGE. Not at all. Cynthia Karslake divorced her husband.

SUDLEY. (*Gloomily, since he has less fault to find than he expected.*) She divorced him! Ah! (*Sips his tea.*)

MISS HENEAGE. The suit went by default. And, my dear William, there are many palliating circumstances. Cynthia was married to Karslake only seven months. There are no— (*Glances at* GRACE.) no hostages to Fortune! Ahem!

SUDLEY. (*Still unwilling to be pleased.*) Ah! What sort of a young woman is she? (*Goes to* C.)

GRACE. (*With the superiority of one who is not too popular.*) Men admire her.

MISS HENEAGE. She's not conventional.

MRS. PHILLIMORE. (*Showing a faint sense of justice.*) I am bound to say she has behaved discreetly ever since she arrived in this house.

MISS HENEAGE. Yes, Mary—but I sometimes suspect that she exercises a degree of self-control—

SUDLEY. (*Glad to have something against some one.*) She claps on the lid, eh? And you think that perhaps some day she'll boil over? Well, of course fifteen or twenty millions—but who's Karslake?

GRACE. (*Very superciliously.*) He owns Cynthia K. She's the famous mare.

MISS HENEAGE. He's Henry Karslake's son.

SUDLEY. (*Beginning to make the best of fifteen millions-in-law.*) Oh!—Henry!—Very respectable family. Although I remember his father served a term in the senate. And so the wedding is to be to-morrow?

MRS. PHILLIMORE. (*Assents.*) To-morrow.

SUDLEY. (*Bored, and his respectability to the front when he thinks of the ceremony; rises.* GRACE *rises.*) To-morrow. Well, my dear Sarah, a respectable family with some means. We must accept her. But on the whole, I think it will be best for me not to see the young woman. My disapprobation would make itself apparent.

GRACE. (*Whispering to* SUDLEY.) Cynthia's coming. (*He doesn't hear.*)

(*Enter* CYNTHIA, *absorbed in reading a newspaper. She is a young creature in her twenties, small and highbred, full of the love of excitement and sport. Her manner is wide awake and keen and she is evidently in no fear of the opinion of others. Her dress is exceedingly elegant, but with the elegance of a woman whose chief interests lie in life out of doors. There is nothing horsey in her style, and her expression is youthful and ingenuous.*)

SUDLEY. (*Sententious and determinately epigrammatic.*) The uncouth modern young woman, eight feet high, with a skin like a rhinoceros and manners like a cave dweller—an habitué of the race-track and the divorce court—

GRACE. (*Aside to* SUDLEY.) Cousin William!

SUDLEY. Eh, oh!

CYNTHIA. (*Comes down reading, immersed, excited, trembling. She lowers paper to catch the light.*) "Belmont favorite—six to one—Rockaway—Rosebud, and Flying Cloud. Slow track—raw wind—hm, hm, hm—At the half, Rockaway forged ahead, when Rosebud under the lash made a bold bid for victory—neck by neck—for a quarter—when Flying Cloud slipped by the pair and won on the post by a nose in one forty nine!" (*To* R. *Speaks with the enthusiasm of a sport.*) Oh, I wish I'd seen the dear thing do it. Oh, it's Mr. Sudley! You must think me very rude. How do you do, Mr. Sudley? (*Goes to* SUDLEY, L. C.)

SUDLEY. (*Very respectable as he bows without cordiality.*) Mrs. Karslake. (*Pause;* CYNTHIA *feels he should say something. As he says nothing, she speaks again.*)

CYNTHIA. I hope Cairo was delightful? Did you have a smooth voyage?

SUDLEY. (*Pompously.*) You must permit me, Mrs. Karslake—

CYNTHIA. (*With good temper, somewhat embarrassed, and talking herself into ease.*) Oh, please don't welcome me to the family. All that formal part is over, if you don't mind. I'm one of the tribe now! You're coming to our wedding to-morrow?

SUDLEY. My dear Mrs. Karslake, I think it might be wiser—

CYNTHIA. (*Still with cordial good temper.*) Oh, but you must come! I mean to be a perfect wife to Philip and all his relations! That sounds rather miscellaneous, but you know what I mean.

SUDLEY. (*Very sententious.*) I am afraid—

CYNTHIA. (*Gay and still covering her embarrassment.*) If you don't come, it'll look as if you were not standing by Philip when he's in trouble! You'll come, won't you—but of course you will.

SUDLEY. (*After a self-important pause.*) I will come, Mrs. Karslake. (*Pause.*) Good-afternoon. (*In a tone of sorrow and compassion.*) Good-bye, Mary. Good-afternoon, Sarah. (*Sighs.*) Grace, dear. (*To* MISS HENEAGE.) At what hour did you say the alimony commences?

MISS HENEAGE. (*Quickly and commandingly to cover his slip. Going up* C.) The ceremony is at three P. M., William. (SUDLEY *goes up* L.)

MRS. PHILLIMORE. (*With fatigued voice and manner as she rises.*) I am going to my room to rest awhile. (MRS. PHILLIMORE *goes up.*)

MISS HENEAGE. (*To* SUDLEY.) Oh, William, one moment—I entirely forgot! I've a most important social question to ask you! (*She goes up slowly to the door with him.*) In regard to the announcements of the wedding—who they shall be sent to and who not. For instance—the Dudleys— (*Exeunt* SUDLEY *and* MISS HENEAGE, *talking.*)

CYNTHIA. (*Sitting on the sofa,* L.) So that's Cousin William?

GRACE. (*Near the tea-table.*) Don't you like him?

CYNTHIA. (*Calmly sarcastic.*) Like him? I love him. He's so generous. He couldn't have received me with more warmth if I'd been a mulatto.

(*Reënter* THOMAS. *Enter* PHILLIMORE. PHILIP PHILLIMORE *is a self-centered, short-tempered, imperious member of the respectable fashionables of New York. He is well and solidly dressed and in manner and speech evidently a man of family. He is accustomed to being listened to in his home circle and from the bench, and it is practically impossible for him to believe that he can make a mistake.*)

GRACE. (*Outraged.*) Really you know— (CYNTHIA *crosses and sits at table.*) Philip! (PHILIP *nods to her absent-mindedly. He is in his working suit and looks tired. He comes down silently, crosses to tea-table. Bends over and kisses* CYNTHIA *on forehead. Goes to his chair, which* THOMAS *has changed the position of for him. Sits, and sighs with satisfaction.*)

PHILIP. (*As if exhausted by brain work.*) Ah, Grace! (*Exit* GRACE.) Well, my dear, I thought I should never extricate myself from the court room. You look very debonnair!

CYNTHIA. The tea's making. You'll have your glass of sherry?

PHILIP. (*The strain of the day having evidently been severe.*) Thanks! (*Takes it from* THOMAS; *sighs.*) Ah!

CYNTHIA. I can see it's been a tiring day with you.

PHILIP. (*As before.*) Hm! (*Sips.*)
CYNTHIA. Were the lawyers very long winded?
PHILIP. (*Almost too tired for speech.*) Prolix to the point of somnolence. It might be affirmed without inexactitude that the prolixity of counsel is the somnolence of the judiciary. I am fatigued, ah! (*A little suddenly, awaking to the fact that his orders have not been carried out to the letter.*) Thomas! My *Post* is not in its usual place!
CYNTHIA. (*To* THOMAS.) It's here, Philip. (THOMAS *gets it.*)
PHILIP. Thanks, my dear. (*Opens "Post."*) Ah! This hour with you—is—is really the—the— (*absently*) the one vivid moment of the day. (*Reading.*) Hm—shocking attack by the president on vested interests. Hm—too bad—but it's to be expected. The people insisted on electing a desperado to the presidential office—they must take the hold-up that follows. (*Pause; he reads.*) Hm! His English is lacking in idiom, his spelling in conservatism, his mind in balance, and his character in repose.
CYNTHIA. (*Amiable but not very sympathetic.*) You seem more fatigued than usual. Another glass of sherry, Philip?
PHILIP. Oh, I ought not to—
CYNTHIA. I think you seem a little more tired than usual.
PHILIP. Perhaps I am. (*She pours out sherry.* PHILIP *takes glass but does not sip.*) Ah, this hour is truly a grateful form of restful excitement. (*Pause.*) You, too, find it—eh? (*Looks at* CYNTHIA.)
CYNTHIA. (*With veiled sarcasm.*) Decidedly.
PHILIP. Decidedly what, my dear?
CYNTHIA. (*As before.*) Restful.
PHILIP. Hm! Perhaps I need the calm more than you do. Over the case to-day I actually—eh— (*sips*) slum-

bered. I heard myself do it. That's how I know. A dressmaker sued on seven counts. (*Reads newspaper.*) Really, the insanity of the United States Senate—you seem restless, my dear. Ah—um—have you seen the evening paper? I see there has been a lightning change in the style or size of hats which ladies— (*He sweeps a descriptive motion with his hand, gives paper to* CYNTHIA, *then moves his glass, reads, and sips.*)

CYNTHIA. The lamp, Thomas. (THOMAS *blows out the alcohol lamp on the tea-table with difficulty. Blows twice. Movement of* PHILIP *each time. Blows again.*)

PHILIP. (*Irritably.*) Confound it, Thomas! What are you puffing and blowing at—?

THOMAS. It's out, ma'am—yes, sir.

PHILIP. You're excessively noisy, Thomas!

THOMAS. (*In a fluster.*) Yes, sir—I am.

CYNTHIA. (*Soothing* THOMAS'S *wounded feelings.*) We don't need you, Thomas.

THOMAS. Yes, ma'am.

PHILIP. Puffing and blowing and shaking and quaking like an automobile in an ecstasy!

(*Exit* THOMAS, L.)

CYNTHIA. (*Not unsympathetically.*) Too bad, Philip! I hope my presence isn't too agitating?

PHILIP. Ah—it's just because I value this hour with you, Cynthia—this hour of tea and toast and tranquillity. It's quite as if we were married—happily married—already.

CYNTHIA. (*Admitting that married life is a blank, begins to look through paper.*) Yes, I feel as if we were married already.

PHILIP. (*Not recognizing her tone.*) Ah! It's the calm, you see.

CYNTHIA. (*As before.*) The calm? Yes—yes, it's—it's the calm.

PHILIP. (*Sighs.*) Yes, the calm—the Halcyon calm of —of second choice. Hm! (*He reads and turns over leaves of paper.* CYNTHIA *reads. Pause.*) After all, my dear— the feeling which I have for you—is—is—eh—the market is in a shocking condition of plethora! Hm—hm—and what are you reading?

CYNTHIA. (*Embarrassed.*) Oh, eh—well—I—eh—I'm just running over the sporting news.

PHILIP. Oh! (*He looks thoughtful.*)

CYNTHIA. (*Beginning to forget* PHILIP *and to remember more interesting matters.*) I fancied Hermes would come in an easy winner. He came in nowhere. Nonpareil was ridden by Henslow—he's a rotten bad rider. He gets nervous.

PHILIP. (*Reading still.*) Does he? Hm! I suppose you do retain an interest in horses and races. Hm—I trust some day the—ah—law will attract—Oh (*turning a page*), here's the report of my opinion in that dressmaker's case—Haggerty *vs.* Phillimore.

CYNTHIA. Was the case brought against you? (*Puzzled.*)

PHILIP. Oh—no. The suit was brought by Haggerty, Miss Haggerty, a dressmaker, against the—in fact, my dear, against the former Mrs. Phillimore. (*Pause; he reads.*)

CYNTHIA. (*Curious about the matter.*) How did you decide it?

PHILIP. I was obliged to decide in Mrs. Phillimore's favor. Haggerty's plea was preposterous.

CYNTHIA. Did you—did you meet the—the—former—?

PHILIP. No.

CYNTHIA. I often see her at afternoon teas.

PHILIP. How did you recognize—

CYNTHIA. Why— (*Opens paper.*) because Mrs. Vida Phillimore's picture appears in every other issue of most of the evening papers. And I must confess I was curious. But, I'm sure you find it very painful to meet her again.

PHILIP. (*Slowly, considering.*) No,—would you find it so impossible to meet Mr.—

CYNTHIA. (*Much excited and aroused.*) Philip! Don't speak of him. He's nothing. He's a thing of the past. I never think of him. I forget him!

PHILIP. (*Somewhat sarcastic.*) That's extraordinarily original of you to forget him.

CYNTHIA. (*Gently, and wishing to drop the subject.*) We each of us have something to forget, Philip—and John Karslake is to me—Well, he's dead!

PHILIP. As a matter of fact, my dear, he *is* dead, or the next thing to it—for he's bankrupt. (*Pause.*)

CYNTHIA. Bankrupt? (*Excited and moved.*) Let's not speak of him. I mean never to see him or think about him or even hear of him! (*He assents. She reads her paper. He sips his tea and reads his paper. She turns a page, starts and cries out.*)

PHILIP. God bless me!

CYNTHIA. It's a picture of—of—

PHILIP. John Karslake?

CYNTHIA. Picture of him, and one of me, and in the middle between us "Cynthia K!"

PHILIP. "Cynthia K?"

CYNTHIA. (*Excited.*) My pet riding mare! The best horse he has! She's an angel even in a photograph! Oh! (*Reading.*) "John Karslake drops a fortune at Saratoga." (*Rises and goes up and down excitedly.* PHILIP *takes paper and reads.*)

PHILIP. (*Unconcerned, as the matter hardly touches him.*) Hem—ah—Advertises country place for sale— stables, famous mare "Cynthia K"—favorite riding-mare of former Mrs. Karslake who is once again to enter the arena of matrimony with the well known and highly respected judge of—

CYNTHIA. (*Sensitive and much disturbed.*) Don't! Don't, Philip, please don't!

PHILIP. My dear Cynthia—take another paper—here's my *Post!* You'll find nothing disagreeable in the *Post.* (CYNTHIA *takes paper.*)

CYNTHIA. (*After reading, sits* L., *near table.*) It's much worse in the *Post.* "John Karslake sells the former Mrs. Karslake's jewels—the famous necklace now at Tiffany's, and the sporty ex-husband sells his wife's portrait by Sargent!" Philip, I can't stand this. (*Puts paper on table* L.)

PHILIP. Really, my dear, Mr. Karslake is bound to appear occasionally in print—or even you may have to meet him.

(*Enter* THOMAS, L. *to* C.)

CYNTHIA. (*Determined and distressed.*) I won't meet him! I won't meet him. Every time I hear his name or "Cynthia K's" I'm so depressed.

THOMAS. (*Announcing with something like reluctance. To* C.) Sir, Mr. Fiddler. Mr. Karslake's trainer.

(*Enter* FIDDLER. *He is an English horse trainer, a wide-awake stocky well-groomed little cockney. He knows his own mind and sees life altogether through a stable door. Well-dressed for his station, and not too young.*)

CYNTHIA. (*Excited and disturbed.*) Fiddler? Tim Fiddler? His coming is outrageous!

FIDDLER. A note for you, sir.

CYNTHIA. (*Impulsively.*) Oh, Fiddler—is that you?
FIDDLER. Yes'm!
CYNTHIA. (*In a half-whisper, still speaking on impulse.*) How is she! Cynthia K? How's Planet II and the colt and Golden Rod? How's the whole stable? Are they well?
FIDDLER. No'm—we're all on the bum. (*Aside.*) Ever since you kicked us over!
CYNTHIA. (*Reproving him, though pleased.*) Fiddler!
FIDDLER. The horses is just simply gone to Egypt since you left, and so's the guv'nor.
CYNTHIA. (*Putting an end to* FIDDLER.) That will do, Fiddler.
FIDDLER. I'm waiting for an answer, sir.
CYNTHIA. What is it, Philip?
PHILIP. (*Uncomfortable.*) A mere matter of business. (*Aside to* FIDDLER.) The answer is, Mr. Karslake can come. The—the coast will be clear. (FIDDLER *exits* L.)
CYNTHIA. (*Amazed; rises.*) You're not going to see him?
PHILIP. But Karslake, my dear, is an old acquaintance of mine. He argues cases before me. I will see that you do not have to meet him. (CYNTHIA *crosses in excited dejection.*)

(*Enter* MATTHEW. *He is a high church clergyman to a highly fashionable congregation. His success is partly due to his social position and partly to his elegance of speech, but chiefly to his inherent amiability, which leaves the sinner in happy peace and smiles on the just and unjust alike.*)

MATTHEW. (*Most amiably.*) Ah, my dear brother!
PHILIP. Matthew. (*Greets him* C.)
MATTHEW. (*Nods to* PHILIP.) Good afternoon, my

dear Cynthia. How charming you look! (CYNTHIA *sits at tea-table. To* CYNTHIA.) Ah, why weren't you in your pew yesterday? I preached a most original sermon. (*Goes up and takes hat and cane to divan.*)

THOMAS. (*Aside to* PHILIP.) Sir, Mrs. Vida Phillimore's maid called you up on the telephone, and you're to expect Mrs. Phillimore on a matter of business.

PHILIP. (*Astonished and disgusted.*) Here, impossible! (*To* CYNTHIA.) Excuse me, my dear! (*Exit* PHILIP, *much embarrassed, followed by* THOMAS.)

MATTHEW. (*Comes down to chair, happily and pleasantly self-important.*) No, really, it was a wonderful sermon, my dear. My text was from Paul—"It is better to marry than to burn." It was a strictly logical sermon. I argued—that, as the grass withereth, and the flower fadeth,—there is nothing final in Nature; not even Death! And, as there is nothing final in Nature, not even Death;—so then if Death is not final—why should marriage be final? (*Gently.*) And so the necessity of—eh—divorce! You see? It was an exquisite sermon! All New York was there! And all New York went away happy! Even the sinners—if there were any! I don't often meet sinners—do you?

CYNTHIA. (*Indulgently, in spite of his folly, because he is kind.*) You're such a dear, delightful Pagan! Here's your tea!

MATTHEW. (*Takes tea.*) Why, my dear—you have a very sad expression!

CYNTHIA. (*A little bitterly.*) Why not?

MATTHEW. (*With sentimental sweetness.*) I feel as if I were of no use in the world when I see sadness on a young face. Only sinners should feel sad. You have committed no sin!

CYNTHIA. (*Impulsively.*) Yes, I have!

MATTHEW. Eh?

CYNTHIA. I committed the unpardonable sin—whe—when I married for love!

MATTHEW. One must not marry for anything else, my dear!

CYNTHIA. Why am I marrying your brother?

MATTHEW. I often wonder why? I wonder why you didn't choose to remain a free woman.

CYNTHIA. (*Going over the ground she has often argued with herself.*) I meant to; but a divorcée has no place in society. I felt horridly lonely! I wanted a friend. Philip was ideal as a friend—for months. Isn't it nice to bind a friend to you?

MATTHEW. Yes—yes! (*Puts down teacup.*)

CYNTHIA. (*Growing more and more excited and moved as she speaks.*) To marry a friend—to marry on prudent, sensible grounds—a man—like Philip? That's what I should have done first, instead of rushing into marriage—because I had a wild, mad, sensitive, sympathetic—passion and pain and fury—of, I don't know what—that almost strangled me with happiness!

MATTHEW. (*Amiable and reminiscent.*) Ah—ah—in my youth—I,—I too!

CYNTHIA. (*Coming back to her manner of every day.*) And besides—the day Philip asked me I was in the dumps! And now—how about marrying only for love?

(*Reënter* PHILIP.)

MATTHEW. Ah, my dear, love is not the only thing in the world!

PHILIP. (*Half aside.*) I got there too late, she'd hung up. (*Up* C.)

CYNTHIA. Who, Philip?

PHILIP. Eh—a lady—eh—

(*Enter* THOMAS, *flurried, with card on salver.*)

THOMAS. A card for you, sir. Ahem—ahem—Mrs. Phillimore—that was, sir.

PHILIP. Eh?

THOMAS. She's on the stairs, sir. (*Turns. Enter* VIDA. THOMAS *announces her as being the best way of meeting the difficulty.*) Mrs. Vida Phillimore!

(VIDA *comes in slowly, with the air of a spoiled beauty. She stops just inside the door and speaks in a very casual manner. Her voice is languourous and caressing. She is dressed in the excess of the French fashion and carries an outré parasol. She smiles and comes, undulating, down* C. *Tableau. Exit* THOMAS.)

VIDA. How do you do, Philip. (*Comes down* C.) Don't tell me I'm a surprise! I had you called up on the 'phone and I sent up my card—and, besides, Philip dear, when you have the—the—habit of the house, as unfortunately I have, you can't treat yourself like a stranger in a strange land. At least, I can't—so here I am. My reason for coming was to ask you about that B. and O. stock we hold in common. (*To* MATTHEW, *condescendingly, the clergy being a class of unfortunates debarred by profession from the pleasures of the world.*) How do you do? (*Pause. She then goes to the real reason of her visit.*) Do be polite and present me to your wife-to-be.

PHILIP. (*Awkwardly.*) Cynthia—

CYNTHIA. (*Comes down to table* R. *of it. Cheerfully, with dash.*) We're delighted to see you, Mrs. Phillimore. I needn't ask you to make yourself at home, but will you have a cup of tea?

(MATTHEW *sits near little table.*)

VIDA. (*To* PHILIP.) My dear, she's not in the least what I expected. I heard she was a dove! She's a **very** dashing kind of a dove! (*To* CYNTHIA; *comes to tea-table.*) My dear, I'm paying you compliments. Five lumps and quantities of cream. I find single life very thinning. (*To* PHILIP, *very calm and ready to be agreeable to any man.*) And how well you're looking! It must be the absence of matrimonial cares—or is it a new angel in the house?

CYNTHIA. (*Outraged at* VIDA'S *intrusion, but polite though delicately sarcastic.*) It's most amusing to sit in your place. And how at home you must feel here in this house where you have made so much trouble—I mean tea. (*Rises.*) Do you know it would be in much better taste if you would take the place you're accustomed to?

VIDA. (*As calm as before.*) My dear, I'm an intruder only for a moment; I shan't give you a chance to score off me again! But I must thank you, dear Philip, for rendering that decision in my favor—

PHILIP. I assure you—

VIDA. (*Unable to resist a thrust at the close of this speech.*) Of course, you would like to have rendered it against me. It was your wonderful sense of justice, and that's why I'm so grateful—if not to you, to your Maker!

PHILIP. (*He feels that this is no place for his future wife. Rises quickly, goes up* C. *To* CYNTHIA.) Cynthia, I would prefer that you left us.

(MATTHEW *comes to* L. *sofa and sits.*)

CYNTHIA. (*Determined not to leave the field first, remains seated.*) Certainly, Philip!

PHILIP. I expect another visitor who—

VIDA. (*With flattering insistence, to* CYNTHIA.) Oh, my dear—don't go! (PHILIP *goes up* L. C.) The truth is—I came to see you! I feel most cordially towards you—and really, you know, people in our position should meet on cordial terms.

CYNTHIA. (*Taking it with apparent calm, but pointing her remarks.*) Naturally. If people in our position couldn't meet, New York society would soon come to an end.

(*Enter* THOMAS.)

VIDA. (*Calm, but getting her knife in too.*) Precisely. Society's no bigger than a band-box. Why, it's only a moment ago I saw Mr. Karslake walking—
CYNTHIA. Ah!
THOMAS. (*Announcing clearly. Every one changes place, in consternation, amusement or surprise.* CYNTHIA *moves to leave the stage, but stops for fear of attracting* KARSLAKE'S *attention.*) Mr. John Karslake!

(*Enter* KARSLAKE. *He is a powerful, generous personality, a man of affairs, breezy, gay and careless. He gives the impression of being game for any fate in store for him. His clothes indicate sporting propensities and his taste in waistcoats and ties is brilliant.* KARSLAKE *sees first* PHILIP *and then* MATTHEW. *Exit* THOMAS.

PHILIP. How do you do?
JOHN. (*Very gay and no respecter of persons.*) Good-afternoon, Mr. Phillimore. Hello—here's the church! (*Crosses to* MATTHEW *and shakes hands. He slaps him on the back.*) I hadn't the least idea—how are you? By George, your reverence, that was a racy sermon of yours on Divorce! What was your text? (*Sees* VIDA *and bows, very politely.*) Galatians 4:2: "The more the merrier," or "Who next?" (*Smiles.*) As the whale said after Jonah!

(CYNTHIA *makes a sudden movement, turns, turns cup over.* JOHN *faces about quickly and they face each other.* JOHN *gives a frank start. Pause. Tableau.*)

JOHN. (*Astounded, in a low voice.*) Mrs. Karslake— (*Bows.*) I was not aware of the pleasure in store for me. I understood you were in the country. (*Recovers, crosses to chair.*) Perhaps you'll be good enough to make me a cup of tea?—that is if the teapot wasn't lost in the scrimmage. (*Pause.* CYNTHIA, *determined to equal him in coolness, returns to the tea-tray.*) Mr. Phillimore, I came to get your signature in that matter of Cox *vs.* Keely.

PHILIP. I shall be at your service, but pray be seated. (*He indicates chair up table.*)

JOHN. (*Sitting beyond but not far from the tea-table.*) And I also understood you to say you wanted a saddle horse. (*Sits* R. *corner.*)

PHILIP. You have a mare called—eh—"Cynthia K"?

JOHN. (*Promptly.*) Yes—she's not for sale.

PHILIP. Oh, but she's just the mare I had set my mind on.

JOHN. (*With a touch of humor.*) You want her for yourself?

PHILIP. (*A little flustered.*) I—eh—I sometimes ride.

JOHN. (*He is sure of himself now.*) She's rather lively for you Judge. Mrs. Karslake used to ride her.

PHILIP. You don't care to sell her to me?

JOHN. She's a dangerous mare, Judge, and she's as delicate and changeable as a girl. I'd hate to leave her in your charge!

CYNTHIA. (*Eagerly but in a low voice.*) Leave her in mine, Mr. Karslake!

JOHN. (*After slight pause.*) Mrs. Karslake knows all about a horse, but— (*Turning to* CYNTHIA.) Cynthia K's got rather tricky of late.

CYNTHIA. (*Haughtily.*) You mean to say you think she'd chuck me?

JOHN. (*With polite solicitude and still humorous. To*

PHILIP.) I'd hate to have a mare of mine deprive you of a wife, Judge. (*Rises.* CYNTHIA *business of anger.*) She goes to Saratoga next week, C. W.

VIDA. (*Who has been sitting and talking to* MATTHEW *for lack of a better man, comes* C. *to talk to* KARSLAKE.) C. W.?

JOHN. (*Rising as she rises.*) Creditors willing.

VIDA. (*Crossing and sitting left of tea-table.*) I'm sure your creditors are willing.

JOHN. Oh, they're a breezy lot, my creditors. They're giving me a dinner this evening.

VIDA. (*More than usually anxious to please.*) I regret I'm not a breezy creditor, but I do think you owe it to me to let me see your Cynthia K! Can't you lead her around to my house?

JOHN. At what hour, Mrs. Phillimore?

VIDA. Say eleven? And you, too, might have a leading in my direction—771 Fifth Avenue. (JOHN *bows.* CYNTHIA *hears and notes this.*)

CYNTHIA. Your cup of tea, Mr. Karslake.

JOHN. Thanks. (JOHN *gets tea and sips.*) I beg your pardon—you have forgotten, Mrs. Karslake—very naturally, it has slipped from your memory, but I don't take sugar. (CYNTHIA, *furious with him and herself. He hands cup back. She makes a second cup.*)

CYNTHIA. (*Cheerfully; in a rage.*) Sorry!

JOHN. (*Also apparently cheerful.*) Yes, gout. It gives me a twinge even to sit in the shadow of a sugar maple! First you riot, and then you diet!

VIDA. (*Calm and amused; aside to* MATTHEW.) My dear Matthew, he's a darling! But I feel as if we were all taking tea on the slope of a volcano! (MATTHEW *sits.*)

PHILIP. It occurred to me, Mr. Karslake, you might be glad to find a purchaser for your portrait by Sargent?

JOHN. It's not *my* portrait. It's a portrait of Mrs.

Karslake, and to tell you the truth—Sargent's a good fellow—I've made up my mind to keep it—to remember the artist by. (CYNTHIA *is wounded by this.*)

PHILIP. Hm!

(CYNTHIA *hands second cup to* JOHN.)

CYNTHIA. (*With careful politeness.*) Your cup of tea, Mr. Karslake.

JOHN. (*Rises; takes tea with courteous indifference.*) Thanks—sorry to trouble you. (*He drinks the cup of tea standing by the tea-table.*)

PHILIP. (*To make conversation.*) You're selling your country place?

JOHN. If I was long of hair—I'd sell that.

CYNTHIA. (*Excited. Taken out of herself by the news.*) You're not really selling your stable?

JOHN. (*Finishes his tea, places empty cup on tea-table and reseats himself.*) Every gelding I've got—seven foals and a donkey! I don't mean the owner.

CYNTHIA. (*Still interested and forgetting the discomfort of the situation.*) How did you ever manage to come such a cropper?

JOHN. Streak of blue luck!

CYNTHIA. (*Quickly.*) I don't see how it's possible—

JOHN. You would if you'd been there. You remember the head man? (*Sits.*) Bloke?

CYNTHIA. Of course!

JOHN. Well, his wife divorced him for beating her over the head with a bottle of Fowler's Solution, and it seemed to prey on his mind. He sold me—

CYNTHIA. (*Horrified.*) Sold a race?

JOHN. About ten races, I guess.

CYNTHIA. (*Incredulous.*) Just because he'd beaten his wife?

JOHN. No. Because she divorced him.

CYNTHIA. Well, I can't see why that should prey on his mind! (*Suddenly remembers.*)

JOHN. Well, I have known men that it stroked the wrong way. But he cost me eighty thousand. And then Urbanity ran third in the thousand dollar stakes for two-year-olds at Belmont.

CYNTHIA. (*She throws this remark in.*) I never had faith in that horse.

JOHN. And, of course, it never rains monkeys but it pours gorillas! So when I was down at St. Louis on the fifth, I laid seven to three on Fraternity—

CYNTHIA. Crazy! Crazy!

JOHN. (*Ready to take the opposite view.*) I don't see it. With her record she ought to have romped it an easy winner.

CYNTHIA. (*Pure sport.*) She hasn't the stamina! Look at her barrel!

JOHN. Well, anyhow, Geranium finished me!

CYNTHIA. You didn't lay odds on Geranium!

JOHN. Why not? She's my own mare—

CYNTHIA. Oh!

JOHN. Streak o' bad luck—

CYNTHIA. (*Plainly anxious to say "I told you so."*) Streak of poor judgment! Do you remember the day you rode Billy at a six foot stone wall, and he stopped and you didn't, and there was a hornet's nest (MATTHEW *rises.*) on the other side, and I remember you were hot just because I said you showed poor judgment? (*She laughs at the memory. A general movement of disapproval. She remembers the situation.*) I beg your pardon.

MATTHEW. (*Rises to meet* VIDA. *Hastily.*) It seems to me that horses are like the fourth gospel. Any conversation about them becomes animated almost beyond the limits of the urbane! (VIDA *disgusted by such plainness of speech, rises and goes to* PHILIP *who waves her to a chair* C.)

PHILIP. (*Formal.*) I regret that you have endured such reverses, Mr. Karslake. (JOHN *quietly bows.*)

CYNTHIA. (*Concealing her interest; speaks casually.*) You haven't mentioned your new English horse—Pantomime. What did he do at St. Louis?

JOHN. (*Sits.*) Fell away and ran fifth.

CYNTHIA. Too bad. Was he fully acclimated? Ah, well—

JOHN. We always differed—you remember—on the time needed—

MATTHEW. (*Coming* C. *to* CYNTHIA, *speaking to carry off the situation as well as to get a tip.*) Isn't there a—eh—a race to-morrow at Belmont Park?

JOHN. Yes. I'm going down in my auto.

CYNTHIA. (*Evidently wishing she might be going too.*) Oh!

MATTHEW. And what animal shall you prefer? (*Covering his personal interest with amiable altruism.*)

JOHN. I'm backing Carmencita.

CYNTHIA. (*Gesture of despair.*) Carmencita! Carmencita!

(MATTHEW *goes to* VIDA.)

JOHN. You may remember we always differed on Carmencita.

CYNTHIA. (*Disgusted at* JOHN'S *dunderheadedness.*) But there's no room for difference. She's a wild, headstrong, dissatisfied, foolish little filly. The deuce couldn't ride her—she'd shy at her own shadow—"Carmencita." Oh, very well then, I'll wager you—and I'll give you odds too—"Decorum" will come in first, and I'll lay three to one he'll beat Carmencita by five lengths! How's that for fair?

JOHN. (*Never forgetting the situation.*) Sorry I'm not flush enough to take you.

CYNTHIA. (*Impetuously.*) Philip, dear, you lend John enough for the wager.

MATTHEW. (*As nearly horrified as so soft a soul can be.*) Ahem! Really—

JOHN. It's a sporty idea, Mrs. Karslake, but perhaps in the circumstances—

CYNTHIA. (*Her mind on her wager.*) In what circumstances?

PHILIP. (*With a nervous laugh.*) It does seem to me there is a certain impropriety—

CYNTHIA. (*Remembering the conventions, which, for a moment, had actually escaped her.*) Oh, I forgot. When horses are in the air—

MATTHEW. (*Pouring oil on troubled waters. Crossing, he speaks to* VIDA *at back of armchair, where she sits.*) It's the fourth gospel, you see.

(*Enter* THOMAS *with letter on salver, which he hands to* PHILIP.)

CYNTHIA. (*Meekly.*) You are quite right, Philip. (PHILIP *goes up.*) The fact is, seeing Mr. Karslake again (*Laying on her indifference with a trowel.*) he seems to me as much a stranger as if I were meeting him for the first time.

MATTHEW. (*Aside to* VIDA.) We are indeed taking tea on the slope of a volcano.

VIDA. (*Is about to go, but thinks she will have a last word with* JOHN.) I'm sorry your fortunes are so depressed, Mr. Karslake.

PHILIP. (*Looking at the card that* THOMAS *has just brought in.*) Who in the world is Sir Wilfrid Cates-Darby? (*General move.*)

JOHN. Oh—eh—Cates-Darby? (PHILIP *opens letter*

which THOMAS *has brought with card.*) That's the English chap I bought Pantomime of.

PHILIP. (*To* THOMAS.) Show Sir Wilfrid Cates-Darby in.

(*Exit* THOMAS. *The prospect of an Englishman with a handle to his name changes* VIDA'S *plans and instead of leaving the house, she goes to sofa,* L. *and sits there.*)

JOHN. He's a good fellow, Judge. Place near Epsom. Breeder. Over here to take a shy at our races.

(*Enter* THOMAS.)

THOMAS. (*Announcing.*) Sir Wilfrid Cates-Darby.

(*Enter* SIR WILFRID CATES-DARBY. *He is a high-bred, sporting Englishman. His manner, his dress and his diction are the perfection of English elegance. His movements are quick and graceful. He talks lightly and with ease. He is full of life and unsmiling good temper.*)

PHILIP. (*To* SIR WILFRID *and referring to the letter of introduction in his hand.*) I am Mr. Phillimore. I am grateful to Stanhope for giving me the opportunity of knowing you, Sir Wilfrid. I fear you find it warm?

SIR WILFRID. (*Delicately mopping his forehead.*) Ah, well—ah—warm, no—hot, yes! Deuced extraordinary climate yours, you know, Mr. Phillimore.

PHILIP. (*Conventional.*) Permit me to present you to— (*The unconventional situation pulls him up short. It takes him a moment to decide how to meet it. He makes up his mind to pretend that everything is as usual, and presents* CYNTHIA *first.*) Mrs. Karslake. (SIR WILFRID *bows, surprised and doubtful.*)

CYNTHIA. How do you do?

PHILIP. And to Mrs. Phillimore. (VIDA *bows nonchalantly, but with a view to catching* SIR WILFRID'S *attention.* SIR WILFRID *bows, and looks from her to* PHILIP.) My brother—and Mr. Karslake you know.

SIR WILFRID. How do, my boy. (*Half aside, to* JOHN.) No idea you had such a charming little wife—What?—Eh?

(KARSLAKE *goes up to speak to* MATTHEW *and* PHILIP *in the further room.*)

CYNTHIA. You'll have a cup of tea, Sir Wilfrid?

SIR WILFRID. (*At table* R.) Thanks, awfully. (*Very cheerfully.*) I'd no idea old John had a wife! The rascal never told me!

CYNTHIA. (*Pouring tea and facing the facts.*) I'm not Mr. Karslake's wife!

SIR WILFRID. Oh!—Eh?—I see— (*Business of thinking it out.*)

VIDA. (*Who has been ready for some time to speak to him.*) Sir Wilfrid, I'm sure no one has asked you how you like our country?

SIR WILFRID. (*Goes to* VIDA *and speaks, standing by her at sofa.*) Oh, well, as to climate and horses, I say nothing. But I like your American humor. I'm acquiring it for home purposes.

VIDA. (*Getting down to love as the basis of conversation.*) Aren't you going to acquire an American girl for home purposes?

SIR WILFRID. The more narrowly I look the agreeable project in the face, the more I like it. Oughtn't to say that in the presence of your husband. (*He casts a look at* PHILIP, *who has gone into the next room.*)

VIDA. (*Cheerful and unconstrained.*) He's not my husband!

SIR WILFRID. (*Completely confused.*) Oh—eh?—my brain must be boiled. You are—Mrs.—eh—ah—of course, now I see! I got the wrong names! I thought you were Mrs. Phillimore. (*He sits by her.*) And that nice girl Mrs. Karslake! You're deucedly lucky to be Mrs. Karslake. John's a prime sort. I say, have you and he got any kids? How many?

VIDA. (*Horrified at being suspected of maternity, but speaking very sweetly.*) He's not my husband.

SIR WILFRID. (*His good spirits all gone, but determined to clear things up.*) Phew! Awfully hot in here! Who the deuce is John's wife?

VIDA. He hasn't any.

SIR WILFRID. Who's Phillimore's wife?

VIDA. He hasn't any.

SIR WILFRID. Thanks, fearfully! (*To* MATTHEW, *whom he approaches; suspecting himself of having lost his wits.*) Would you excuse me, my dear and Reverend Sir—you're a churchman and all that—would you mind straightening me out?

MATTHEW. (*Most gracious.*) Certainly, Sir Wilfrid. Is it a matter of doctrine?

SIR WILFRID. Oh, damme—beg your pardon,—no, it's not words, it's women.

MATTHEW. (*Ready to be outraged.*) Women!

SIR WILFRID. It's divorce. Now, the lady on the sofa—

MATTHEW. *Was* my brother's wife; he divorced her—incompatibility—Rhode Island. The lady at the tea-table *was* Mr. Karslake's wife; she divorced him—desertion—Sioux Falls. One moment—she is about to marry my brother.

Sir Wilfrid. (*Cheerful again.*) I'm out! Thought I never would be! Thanks! (Vida *laughs.*)

Vida. (*Not a whit discountenanced and ready to please.*) Have you got me straightened out yet?

Sir Wilfrid. Straight as a die! I say, you had lots of fun, didn't you? (*Goes back to sofa; stands.*) And so she's Mrs. John Karslake?

Vida. (*Calm, but secretly disappointed.*) Do you like her?

Sir Wilfrid. My word!

Vida. (*Fully expecting personal flattery.*) Eh?

Sir Wilfrid. She's a box o' ginger!

Vida. You haven't seen many American women!

Sir Wilfrid. Oh, haven't I?

Vida. If you'll pay me a visit to-morrow—at twelve, you shall meet a most charming young woman, who has seen you once, and who admires you—ah!

Sir Wilfrid. I'm there—what!

Vida. Seven hundred and seventy-one Fifth Avenue.

Sir Wilfrid. Seven seventy-one Fifth Avenue—at twelve.

Vida. At twelve.

Sir Wilfrid. Thanks! (*Indicates* Cynthia.) She's a thoroughbred—you can see that with one eye shut. Twelve. (*Shakes hands.*) Awfully good of you to ask me. (*Joins* John.) I say, my boy, your former's an absolute certainty. (*To* Cynthia.) I hear you're about to marry Mr. Phillimore, Mrs. Karslake?

(Karslake *crosses to* Vida; *they both go to sofa, left, where they sit.*)

Cynthia. To-morrow, 3 p. m., Sir Wilfrid.

Sir Wilfrid. (*Much taken with* Cynthia. *To her. Sits* R.) Afraid I've run into a sort of family party, eh? (*In-*

dicates VIDA.) The Past and the Future—awfully chic way you Americans have of asking your divorced husbands and wives to drop in, you know—celebrate a christenin', or the new bride, or—

CYNTHIA. Do you like your tea strong?

SIR WILFRID. Middlin'.

CYNTHIA. Sugar?

SIR WILFRID. One!

CYNTHIA. Lemon?

SIR WILFRID. Just torture a lemon over it. (*He makes a gesture as of twisting a lemon peel. She gives tea.*) Thanks! So you do it to-morrow at three?

CYNTHIA. At three, Sir Wilfrid.

SIR WILFRID. Sorry!

CYNTHIA. Why are you sorry?

SIR WILFRID. Hate to see a pretty woman married. Might marry her myself.

CYNTHIA. Oh, but I'm sure you don't admire American women.

SIR WILFRID. Admire you, Mrs. Karslake—

CYNTHIA. Not enough to marry me, I hope.

SIR WILFRID. Marry you in a minute! Say the word. Marry you now—here.

CYNTHIA. You don't think you ought to know me a little before—

SIR WILFRID. Know you? Do know you. (CYNTHIA *covering her hair with her handkerchief.*)

CYNTHIA. What color is my hair?

SIR WILFRID. Pshaw!

CYNTHIA. You see! You don't know whether I'm a chestnut or a strawberry roan! In the States we think a few months of friendship is quite necessary.

SIR WILFRID. Few months of moonshine! Never was a friend to a woman—thank God, in all my life.

CYNTHIA. Oh—oh, oh!

SIR WILFRID. Might as well talk about being a friend to a whiskey and soda.

CYNTHIA. A woman has a soul, Sir Wilfrid.

SIR WILFRID. Well, good whiskey is spirits—dozens o' souls!

CYNTHIA. You are so gross!

SIR WILFRID. (*Changes seat to above table.*) Gross? Not a bit! Friendship between the sexes is all fudge! I'm no friend to a rose in my garden. I don't call it friendship—eh—eh—a warm, starry night, moonbeams and ilex trees, "and a spirit who knows how" and all that—eh— (*Getting closer to her.*) You make me feel awfully poetical, you know— (PHILIP *comes down, glances nervously at* CYNTHIA *and* SIR WILFRID, *and walks up again.*) What's the matter? But, I say—poetry aside—do you, eh— (*Looks around to place* PHILIP.) Does he—y'know—is he—does he go to the head?

CYNTHIA. Sir Wilfrid, Mr. Phillimore is my sober second choice.

SIR WILFRID. Did you ever kiss him? I'll bet he fined you for contempt of court. Look here, Mrs. Karslake, if you're marryin' a man you don't care about—

CYNTHIA. (*Amused and excusing his audacity as a foreigner's eccentricity.*) Really!

SIR WILFRID. Well, I don't offer myself—

CYNTHIA. Oh!

SIR WILFRID. Not this instant—

CYNTHIA. Ah!

SIR WILFRID. But let me drop in to-morrow at ten.

CYNTHIA. What country and state of affairs do you think you have landed in?

SIR WILFRID. New York, by Jove! Been to school, too. New York is bounded on the North, South, East and West by the state of Divorce! Come, come, Mrs. Karslake, I like your country. You've no fear and no respect

—no can't and lots of can. Here you all are, you see—your former husband, and your new husband's former wife—sounds like Ollendoff! Eh? So there you are, you see! But, jokin' apart—why do you marry him? Oh, well, marry him if you must! You can run around the corner and get a divorce afterwards—

CYNTHIA. I believe you think they throw one in with an ice-cream soda!

SIR WILFRID. (*Rises.*) Damme, my dear lady, a marriage in your country is no more than a—eh—eh—what do you call 'em? A thank you, ma'am. That's what an American marriage is—a thank you, ma'am. Bump—bump—you're over it and on to the next.

CYNTHIA. You're an odd fish! What? I believe I like you!

SIR WILFRID. 'Course you do! You'll see me when I call to-morrow—at ten? We'll run down to Belmont Park, eh?

CYNTHIA. Don't be absurd!

VIDA. (*Has finished her talk with* JOHN, *and breaks in on* SIR WILFRID, *who has hung about* CYNTHIA *too long to suit her.*) To-morrow at twelve, Sir Wilfrid!

SIR WILFRID. Twelve! (*Crossing down* L.)

VIDA. (*Shakes hands with* JOHN.) Don't forget, Mr. Karslake—eleven o'clock to-morrow.

JOHN. (*Bows assent.*) I won't!

VIDA. (*Comes to the middle of the stage and speaks to* CYNTHIA.) Oh, Mrs. Karslake, I've ordered Tiffany to send you something. It's a sugar bowl to sweeten the matrimonial lot! I suppose nothing would induce you to call?

CYNTHIA. (*Distant and careless of offending.*) Thanks, no—that is, is "Cynthia K" really to be there at eleven? I'd give a gold mine to see her again.

VIDA. (*Above chair.*) Do come!

ACT I   THE NEW YORK IDEA   41

CYNTHIA. If Mr. Karslake will accommodate me by his absence.

VIDA. Dear Mr. Karslake, you'll have to change your hour.

JOHN. Sorry, I'm not able to.

CYNTHIA. I can't come later for I'm to be married.

JOHN. It's not as bad as that with me, but I am to be sold up—Sheriff, you know. Can't come later than eleven.

VIDA. (*To* CYNTHIA.) Any hour but eleven, dear.

CYNTHIA. (*Perfectly regardless of* VIDA, *and ready to vex* JOHN *if possible.*) Mrs. Phillimore, I shall call on you at eleven—to see Cynthia K. I thank you for the invitation. Good-afternoon.

VIDA. (*Aside to* JOHN, *crossing to speak quietly to him.*) It's mere bravado; she won't come.

JOHN. You don't know her.

(*Pause. General embarrassment.* SIR WILFRID *business with eye-glass.* JOHN *angry.* CYNTHIA *triumphant.* MATTHEW *embarrassed.* VIDA *irritated.* PHILIP *puzzled. Everybody at odds.*)

SIR WILFRID. (*For the first time a witness to the pretty complications of divorce; to* MATTHEW.) Do you have it as warm as this ordinarily?

MATTHEW. (*For whom these moments are more than usually painful, and wiping his brow.*) It's not so much the heat as the humidity.

JOHN. (*Looks at watch; glad to be off.*) I shall be late for my creditors' dinner.

SIR WILFRID. (*Comes down.*) Creditors' dinner.

JOHN. (*Reads note.*) Fifteen of my sporting creditors have arranged to give me a blow-out at Sherry's, and I'm expected right away or sooner. And by the way, I was to bring my friends—if I had any. So now's the time to stand by me! Mrs. Phillimore?

VIDA. Of course!

JOHN. (*Ready to embarrass* CYNTHIA, *if possible, and speaking as if he had quite forgotten their former relations.*) Mrs. Karslake—I beg your pardon. Judge? (PHILIP *declines.*) No? Sir Wilfrid?

SIR WILFRID. I'm with you!

JOHN. (*To* MATTHEW.) Your Grace?

MATTHEW. I regret—

SIR WILFRID. Is it the custom for creditors—

JOHN. Come on, Sir Wilfrid! (THOMAS *opens door.*) Good-night, Judge—Your Grace—

SIR WILFRID. Is it the custom—

JOHN. Hang the custom! Come on—I'll show you a gang of creditors worth having!

(*Exit* SIR WILFRID *with* JOHN, *arm in arm, preceded by* VIDA. MATTHEW *crosses, smiling, as if pleased, in a Christian way, with this display of generous gaiety. Looks at his watch.*)

MATTHEW. Good gracious! I had no idea the hour was so late. I've been asked to a meeting with Maryland and Iowa, to talk over the divorce situation. (*Exit. Voice heard off.*) Good-afternoon! Good-afternoon!

(CYNTHIA *evidently much excited. The outer door slams.* PHILIP *comes down slowly.* CYNTHIA *stands, her eyes wide, her breathing visible, until* PHILIP *speaks, when she seems suddenly to realize her position. A long pause.*)

PHILIP. (*Superior.*) I have seldom witnessed a more amazing cataclysm of jocundity! Of course, my dear, this has all been most disagreeable for you.

CYNTHIA. (*Excitedly.*) Yes, yes, yes!

PHILIP. I saw how much it shocked your delicacy.
CYNTHIA. (*Distressed and moved.*) Outrageous. (PHILIP *sits.*)
PHILIP. Do be seated, Cynthia. (*Takes up paper. Quietly.*) Very odd sort of an Englishman—that Cates-Darby!
CYNTHIA. Sir Wilfrid?—Oh, yes! (PHILIP *settles down to paper. To herself.*) Outrageous! I've a great mind to go at eleven—just as I said I would!
PHILIP. Do sit down, Cynthia!
CYNTHIA. What? What?
PHILIP. You make me so nervous—
CYNTHIA. Sorry—sorry. (*She sits, sees paper, takes it, looks at picture of* JOHN KARSLAKE.)
PHILIP. (*Sighs with content.*) Ah! now that I see him, I don't wonder you couldn't stand him. There's a kind of—ah—spontaneous inebriety about him. He is incomprehensible! If I might with reverence cross question the Creator, I would say to him: "Sir, to what end or purpose did you create Mr. John Karslake?" I believe I should obtain no adequate answer! However (*Sighs.*) at last we have peace—and the *Post!* (PHILIP *settles himself, reads paper;* CYNTHIA *looks at her paper, occasionally looks across at* PHILIP.) Forget the dust of the arena—the prolixity of counsel—the involuntary fatuity of things in general. (*Pause. He reads.*) Compose yourself!

(MISS HENEAGE, MRS. PHILLIMORE *and* GRACE *enter.* CYNTHIA *sighs without letting her sigh be heard. Tries to compose herself. Glances at paper and then hearing* MISS HENEAGE, *starts slightly.* MISS HENEAGE *and* MRS. PHILLIMORE *stop at table.*)

MISS HENEAGE. (*She carries a sheet of paper.*) There, my dear Mary, is the announcement as I have now reworded it. I took William's suggestion. (Mrs. Phillimore *takes and casually reads it.*) I also put the case to him, and he was of the opinion that the announcement should be sent *only* to those people who are really *in* society. (*Sits above table.* Cynthia *braces herself to bear the* Phillimore *conversation.*)

Grace. I wish you'd make an exception of the Dudleys.

(Cynthia *rises and crosses to chair* R. *of* L. *table.*)

Miss Heneage. And, of course, that excludes the Oppenheims—the Vance-Browns.

Mrs. Phillimore. It's just as well to be exclusive.

Grace. I do wish you'd make an exception of Lena Dudley.

Miss Heneage. We might, of course, include those new Girardos, and possibly—possibly the Paddingtons.

Grace. I do wish you would take in Lena Dudley. (*They are now sitting.*)

Mrs. Phillimore. The mother Dudley is as common as a charwoman, and not nearly as clean.

Philip. (*Sighs. His own feelings as usual to the fore.*) Ah! I certainly am fatigued!

(Cynthia *begins to slowly crush the newspaper she has been reading with both hands, as if the effort of self-repression were too much for her.*)

Miss Heneage. (*Making the best of a gloomy future.*) We shall have to ask the Dudleys sooner or later to dine, Mary—because of the elder girl's marriage to that dissolute French Marquis.

Mrs. Phillimore. (*Plaintively.*) I don't like common people any more than I like common cats, and of course in my time—

ACT I THE NEW YORK IDEA 45

Miss Heneage. I think I shall include the Dudleys.

Mrs. Phillimore. You think you'll include the Dudleys?

Miss Heneage. Yes, I think I will include the Dudleys!

(*Here* Cynthia *gives up. Driven desperate by their chatter, she has slowly rolled her newspaper into a ball, and at this point tosses it violently to the floor and bursts into hysterical laughter.*)

Mrs. Phillimore. Why, my dear Cynthia—Compose yourself.

Philip. (*Hastily.*) What is the matter, Cynthia? (*They speak together. General movement.*)

Miss Heneage. Why, Mrs. Karslake, what is the matter?

Grace. (*Comes quickly forward, saying.*) Mrs. Karslake!

CURTAIN

ACT TWO

SCENE: MRS. VIDA PHILLIMORE'S *boudoir. The room is furnished to please an empty-headed, pleasure-loving and fashionable woman. The furniture, the ornaments, what pictures there are, all witness to taste up-to-date. Two French windows open on to a balcony, from which the trees of Central Park can be seen. There is a table between them; a mirror, a scent bottle, etc., upon it. On the right, up stage, is a door; on the right, down stage, another door. A lady's writing table stands between the two, nearer centre of stage. There is another door up stage,* L.; *below it,* L., *an open fireplace, filled with potted plants, and-irons, etc., not in use. Over it a tall mirror; on the mantelpiece a French clock, candelabra, vases, etc. On a line with the fireplace, a lounge, gay with silk pillows. A florist's box, large and long, filled with American Beauty roses, on a low table near the head of the lounge. Small tables and light chairs where needed.*

AT RISE: BENSON *is discovered up stage looking about her. She is a neat and pretty little English lady's maid in black silk and a thin apron. She comes down stage still looking about, goes* L. *and sees flower box; then goes* R., *opens door and speaks off.*

BENSON. Yes, ma'am, the flowers have come. (*She holds the door,* R., *open.* VIDA, *in a morning gown, enters* R., *slowly, and comes* C. *She is smoking a cigarette in as aesthetic a manner as she can, and is evidently turned out in her best style for conquest.*)

VIDA. (C., *back to audience, always calm and, though civil, a little disdainful of her servants.*) Terribly garish light, Benson. Pull down the— (BENSON *obeys.*) Lower still—that will do. (*As she speaks, she goes about the room, giving the furniture a push here and there, arranging vases, etc.*) Men hate a clutter of chairs and tables. (*Stops before table at* C. *and takes up hand mirror, standing with back to audience.*) I really think I'm too pale for this light.

BENSON. (*Quickly, understanding what is implied.*) Yes, ma'am. (BENSON *exits* R. VIDA *sits* C., *table* R. *Knock at door up* L.) Come! (*Enter* BROOKS.)

BROOKS. (*An ultra English footman, in plush and calves.*) Any horders, m'lady?

VIDA. (*Incapable of remembering the last man, or of considering the new one.*) Oh,—of course! You're the new—

BROOKS. Footman, m'lady.

VIDA. (*As a matter of form.*) Your name?

BROOKS. Brooks, m'lady.

(*Reënter* BENSON *with rouge.*)

VIDA. (*Carefully giving instructions while she keeps her eyes on the glass and is rouged by* BENSON.) Brooks, I am at home to Mr. Karslake at eleven, not to any one else till twelve, when I expect Sir Wilfrid Cates-Darby. (BROOKS *is inattentive; watches* BENSON.)

BROOKS. Yes, m'lady.

VIDA. (*Calm, but wearied by the ignorance of the lower classes.*) And I regret to inform you, Brooks, that in America there are no ladies, except salesladies!

BROOKS. (*Without a trace of comprehension.*) Yes, m'lady.

VIDA. I am at home to no one but the two names I have mentioned. (BROOKS *bows and exits up* L. *She dabs on rouge while* BENSON *holds glass.*) Is the men's club room in order?

BENSON. Perfectly, ma'am.

VIDA. Whiskey and soda?

BENSON. Yes, ma'am, and the ticker's been mended. The British sporting papers arrived this morning.

VIDA. (*Looking at her watch which lies on the dressing table.*) My watch has stopped.

BENSON. (*Glancing at the French clock on the chimney-piece.*) Five to eleven, ma'am. (*Comes down a little,* R.)

VIDA. (*Getting promptly to work.*) Hm, hm, I shall be caught. (*Rises and crosses* R.) The box of roses, Benson! (BENSON *brings the box of roses, uncovers the flowers and places them at* VIDA'S *side.*) My gloves—the clippers, and the vase! (*Each of these things* BENSON *places in turn within* VIDA'S *range where she sits on the sofa. She has the long box of roses at her side on a small table, a vase of water on the floor by her side. She cuts the stems and places the roses in the vase. When she feels that she has reached a picturesque position, in which any onlooker would see in her a creature filled with the love of flowers and of her fellow man, she says:*) There! (*The door opens and* BROOKS *enters;* VIDA *nods to* BENSON.)

BROOKS. (*Announcing stolidly.*) Sir John Karslake. (*Enter* JOHN, *dressed in very nobby riding togs, crop, etc., and spurs. He comes in gaily and forcibly.* BENSON *gives way,* R., *as he comes down. Exeunt* BROOKS *and* BENSON. JOHN *stops near table,* L. VIDA, *from this point on, is busied with her roses.*)

VIDA. (*Langourously, but with a faint suggestion of humor.*) Is that really you, Sir John?

JOHN. (*Lively and far from being impressed by* VIDA.) I see now where we Americans are going to get our titles. Good-morning! You look as fresh as paint. (*Takes chair from* L. *to* R. C.)

VIDA. (*Facing the insinuation with gentle pain.*) I hope you don't mean that? I never flattered myself for a moment you'd come. You're riding Cynthia K?

JOHN. (*Who has laid his gloves and riding crop on table,* C.) Fiddler's going to lead her round here in ten minutes!

VIDA. Cigars and cigarettes! Scotch? (*She indicates that he will find them on a small table up stage.*)

JOHN. Scotch! (*Goes up quickly to table and helps himself to Scotch and seltzer.*)

VIDA. And now *do* tell me all about *her!* (*Putting in her last roses; she keeps one rosebud in her hand, of a size suitable for a man's buttonhole.*)

JOHN. (*As he drinks.*) Oh, she's an adorable creature—delicate, high-bred, sweet-tempered—

VIDA. (*Showing her claws for a moment.*) Sweet-tempered? Oh, you're describing the horse! By "her," I meant—

JOHN. (*Irritated by the remembrance of his wife.*) Cynthia Karslake? I'd rather talk about the last Tornado. (*Sits.*)

VIDA. (*Soothing the savage beast.*) There is only one thing I want to talk about, and that is, *you!* Why were you unhappy?

JOHN. (*Still cross.*) Why does a dollar last such a short time?

VIDA. (*Curious.*) Why did you part?

JOHN. Did you ever see a schooner towed by a tug? Well, I parted from Cynthia for the same reason that the hawser parts from the tug—I couldn't stand the tug.

VIDA. (*Sympathizing.*) Ah! (*Pause.*)

JOHN. (*Still cross.*) Awful cheerful morning chat.

VIDA. (*Excusing her curiosity and coming back to love as the only subject for serious conversation.*) I must hear the story, for I'm anxious to know why I've taken such a fancy to you!

JOHN. (*Very nonchalantly.*) Why do *I* like you?

VIDA. (*Doing her best to charm.*) I won't tell you—it would flatter you too much.

JOHN. (*Not a bit impressed by* VIDA, *but as ready to flirt as another.*) Tell me!

VIDA. There's a rose for you. (*Giving him the one she has in her hand.*)

JOHN. (*Saying what is plainly expected of him.*) I want more than a rose—

VIDA. (*Putting this insinuation by.*) You refuse to tell me—?

JOHN. (*Once more reminded of* CYNTHIA, *speaks with sudden feeling.*) There's nothing to tell. We met, we loved, we married, we parted; or at least we wrangled and jangled. (*Sighs.*) Ha! Why weren't we happy? Don't ask me, why! It may have been *partly* my fault!

VIDA. (*With tenderness.*) Never!

JOHN. (*His mind on* CYNTHIA.) But I believe it's all in the way a girl's brought up. Our girls are brought up to be ignorant of life—they're ignorant of life. Life is a joke, and marriage is a picnic and a man is a shawl-strap—'Pon my soul, Cynthia Deane—no, I can't tell you! (*Rises and goes up. During the following, he walks about in his irritation.*)

VIDA. (*Gently.*) Please tell me!

JOHN. Well, she was an heiress, an American heiress—and she'd been taught to think marriage meant burnt almonds and moonshine and a yacht and three automobiles, and she thought—I don't know what she thought, but I tell you, Mrs. Phillimore, marriage is three

ACT II THE NEW YORK IDEA 51

parts love and seven parts forgiveness of sins. (*Crosses
c.*)

VIDA. (*Flattering him as a matter of course.*) She never loved you.

JOHN. (*On whom she has made no impression at all.*) Yes, she did. For six or seven months there was not a shadow between us. It was perfect, and then one day she went off like a pistol-shot! I had a piece of law work and couldn't take her to see Flashlight race the Maryland mare. The case meant a big fee, big Kudos, and in sails Cynthia, Flashlight mad! And will I put on my hat and take her? No—and bang she goes off like a stick o' dynamite—what did I marry her for?—and words— pretty high words, until she got mad, when she threw over a chair and said oh, well,—marriage was a failure, or it was with me, so I said she'd better try somebody else. She said she would, and marched out of the room. (*Back to L.*)

VIDA. (*Gently sarcastic.*) But she came back!

JOHN. She came back, but not as you mean. She stood at the door and said, "Jack, I shall divorce you." Then she came over to my study-table, dropped her wedding ring on my law papers, and went out. The door shut, I laughed; the front door slammed, I damned. (*Pause; crosses to window.*) She never came back. (*Goes up, then comes down to chair R. VIDA catches his hands.*)

VIDA. (*Hoping for a contradiction.*) She's broken your heart.

JOHN. Oh, no! (*Crosses to chair by lounge.*)

VIDA. (*Encouraged, begins to play the game again.*) You'll never love again!

JOHN. (*Speaking to her from the foot of her sofa.*) Try me! Try me! Ah, no, Mrs. Phillimore, I shall laugh, live, love and make money again! And let me tell you one thing—I'm going to rap her one over the knuckles. She had a stick of a Connecticut lawyer, and he—well, to cut a legal story short, since Mrs. Karslake's been in Europe, I have been quietly testing the validity of the decree of divorce. Perhaps you don't understand?

VIDA. (*Letting her innate shrewdness appear.*) Oh, about a divorce, everything!

JOHN. I shall hear by this evening whether the divorce will stand or not.

VIDA. But it's to-day at three she marries—you won't let her commit bigamy?

JOHN. (*Shakes his head.*) I don't suppose I'd go as far as that. It may be the divorce will hold, but anyway I hope never to see her again. (*He sits beside her facing up stage as she faces down.*)

VIDA. Ah, my poor boy, she has broken your heart. (*Believing that this is her psychological moment, she lays her hand on his arm, but draws it back as soon as he attempts to take it.*) Now don't make love to me.

JOHN. (*Bold and amused, but never taken in.*) Why not?

VIDA. (*With immense gentleness.*) Because I like you too much! (*More gaily.*) I might give in, and take a notion to like you still more!

JOHN. Please do!

VIDA. (*With gush and determined to be womanly at all hazards.*) Jack, I believe you'd be a lovely lover!

JOHN. (*As before.*) Try me!

VIDA. (*Not hoping much from his tone.*) You charming, tempting, delightful fellow, I could love you without the least effort in the world,—but, no!

JOHN. (*Playing the game.*) Ah, well, now *seriously!* Between two people who have *suffered* and made their own mistakes—

VIDA. (*Playing the game too, but not playing it well.*) But you see, you don't *really* love me!

JOHN. (*Still ready to say what is expected.*) Cynthia—Vida, no man can sit beside you and look into your eyes without feeling—

VIDA. (*Speaks the truth as she sees it, seeing that her methods don't succeed.*) Oh! That's not love! That's simply—well, my dear Jack, it's beginning at the wrong end. And the truth is you hate Cynthia Karslake with such a whole-hearted hate, that you haven't a moment to think of any other woman.

JOHN. (*With sudden anger.*) I hate her!

VIDA. (*Very softly and most sweetly.*) Jack—Jack, I could be as foolish about you as—oh, as foolish as anything, my dear! And perhaps some day—perhaps some day you'll come to me and say, Vida, I am totally indifferent to Cynthia—and then—

JOHN. And then?

VIDA. (*The ideal woman in mind.*) Then, perhaps, you and I may join hands and stroll together into the Garden of Eden. It takes two to find the Garden of Eden, you know—and once we're on the inside, we'll lock the gate.

JOHN. (*Gaily, and seeing straight through her veneer.*) And lose the key under a rose-bush!

VIDA. (*Agreeing very softly.*) Under a rose-bush! (*Very soft knock* R.) Come! (JOHN *rises quickly. Enter* BENSON *and* BROOKS, L.)

BROOKS. (*Stolid and announcing.*) My lady—Sir Wilf— (BENSON *stops him with a sharp movement and turns toward* VIDA.)

BENSON. (*With intention.*) Your dressmaker, ma'am. (BENSON *waves* BROOKS *to go. Exit* BROOKS, L., *very haughtily.*)

VIDA. (*Wonderingly.*) My dressmaker, Benson? (*With quick intelligence.*) Oh, of course, show her up. Mr. Karslake, you won't mind for a few minutes using my men's club room? Benson will show you! You'll find cigars and the ticker, sporting papers, whiskey; and, if you want anything special, just 'phone down to my "chef."

JOHN. (*Looking at his watch.*) How long?

VIDA. (*Very anxious to please.*) Half a cigar! Benson will call you.

JOHN. (*Practical.*) Don't make it too long. You see, there's my sheriff's sale on at twelve, and those races this afternoon. Fiddler will be here in ten minutes, remember! (*Door* L. *opens.*)

VIDA. (*To* JOHN.) Run along! (*Exit* JOHN. VIDA *suddenly practical, and with a broad gesture to* BENSON.) Everything just as it was, Benson! (BENSON *whisks the roses out of the vase and replaces them in the box. She gives* VIDA *scissors and empty vases, and when* VIDA *finds herself in precisely the same position which preceded* JOHN'S *entrance, she says:*) There! (*Enter* BROOKS, *as* VIDA *takes a rose from basket.*)

BROOKS. (*Stolidly.*) Your ladyship's dressmaker! M'lady! (*Enter* SIR WILFRID *in morning suit, boutonniére, etc.*)

VIDA. (*With tender surprise and busy with the roses.*) Is that really you, Sir Wilfrid! I never flattered myself for an instant that you'd remember to come.

SIR WILFRID. (*Coming to her above end of sofa.*) Come? 'Course I come! Keen to come see you. By Jove, you know, you look as pink and white as a huntin' mornin'.

VIDA. (*Ready to make any man as happy as possible.*) You'll smoke?

SIR WILFRID. Thanks! (*He watches her as she trims and arranges the flowers.*) Awfully long fingers you have! Wish I was a rose, or a ring, or a pair of shears! I say, d' you ever notice what a devil of a fellow I am for originality, what? (*Comes down to* L. *Unlike* JOHN, *is evidently impressed by her.*) You've got a delicate little den up here! Not so much low livin' and high thinkin', as low lights and no thinkin' at all, I hope—eh? (*To* C. *By this time* VIDA *has filled a vase with roses and rises to sweep by him and if possible make another charming picture to his eyes.*)

VIDA. You don't mind my moving about? (*Crosses* R.)

SIR WILFRID. (*Impressed.*) Not if you don't mind my watchin'. (*Sits* R., *on sofa.*) And sayin' how well you do it.

VIDA. It's most original of you to come here this morning. I don't quite see why you did. (*She places the roses here and there, as if to see their effect, and leaves them on a small table near the door through which her visitors entered.*)

SIR WILFRID. Admiration.

VIDA. (*Sauntering slowly toward the mirror as she speaks.*) Oh, I saw that you admired her! And of course, she did say she was coming here at eleven! But that was only bravado! She won't come, and besides, I've given orders to admit no one!

SIR WILFRID. May I ask you— (*He throws this in in the middle of her speech, which flows gently and steadily on.*)

VIDA. And indeed, if she came now, Mr. Karslake has gone, and her sole object in coming was to make him uncomfortable. (*Goes up above table,* L.; *stopping a half minute at the mirror to see that she looks as she wishes to look.*) Very dangerous symptom, too, that passionate desire to make one's former husband unhappy! But, I can't believe that your admiration for Cynthia Karslake is so warm that it led you to pay me this visit a half hour too early in the hope of seeing—

SIR WILFRID. (*Rises; most civil, but speaking his mind like a Briton.*) I say, would you mind stopping a moment! (*She smiles.*) I'm not an American, you know; I was brought up not to interrupt. But you Americans, it's different with you! If somebody didn't interrupt you, you'd go on forever.

VIDA. (*She passes him to tantalize.*) My point is you come to see Cynthia—

SIR WILFRID. (*He believes she means it.*) I came hopin' to see—

VIDA. (*As before.*) Cynthia!

SIR WILFRID. (*Perfectly single-minded and entirely taken in.*) But I would have come even if I'd known—

VIDA. (*Crosses* C.) I don't believe it!

SIR WILFRID. (*As before.*) Give you my word I—

VIDA. (*The same.*) You're here to see *her!* And of course—

SIR WILFRID. (*Determined to be heard because, after all, he's a man.*) May I have the—eh—the floor? (VIDA *sits in chair,* L.) I was jolly well bowled over with Mrs. Karslake, I admit that, and I hoped to see her here, but—

VIDA. (*Talking nonsense and knowing it.*) You had another object in coming. In fact, you came to see Cynthia, and you came to see me! What I really long to know, is why you wanted to see *me!* For, of course, Cynthia's to be married at three! And, if she wasn't she wouldn't have you!

SIR WILFRID. (*Not intending to wound; merely speaking the flat truth.*) Well, I mean to jolly well ask her.

VIDA. (*Indignant.*) To be your wife?

SIR WILFRID. (C.) Why not?

VIDA. (*As before.*) And you came here, to my house—in order to ask her—

SIR WILFRID. (*Truthful even on a subtle point.*) Oh, but that's only my first reason for coming, you know.

VIDA. (*Concealing her hopes.*) Well, now I *am* curious—what is the second?

ACT II   THE NEW YORK IDEA   57

SIR WILFRID. (*Simply.*) Are you feelin' pretty robust?
VIDA. I don't know!
SIR WILFRID. (*Crosses* R. *to buffet.*) Will you have something, and then I'll tell you!
VIDA. (*Gaily.*) Can't I support the news without—
SIR WILFRID. (*Trying to explain his state of mind, a thing he has never been able to do.*) Mrs. Phillimore, you see it's this way. Whenever you're lucky, you're too lucky. Now, Mrs. Karslake is a nipper and no mistake, but as I told you, the very same evenin' and house where I saw her— (*He attempts to take her hand.*)
VIDA. (*Gently rising and affecting a tender surprise.*) What!
SIR WILFRID. (*Rising with her.*) That's it!—You're over! (*He suggests with his right hand the movement of a horse taking a hurdle.*)
VIDA. (*Very sweetly.*) You don't really mean—
SIR WILFRID. (*Carried away for the moment by so much true womanliness.*) I mean, I stayed awake for an hour last night, thinkin' about you.
VIDA. (*Speaking to be contradicted.*) But, you've just told me—that Cynthia—
SIR WILFRID. (*Admitting the fact.*) Well, she did—she did bowl my wicket, but so did you—
VIDA. (*Taking him very gently to task.*) Don't you think there's a limit to— (*Sits.*)
SIR WILFRID. (*Roused by so much loveliness of soul.*) Now, see here, Mrs. Phillimore! You and I are not bottle babies, eh, are we? You've been married and—I—I've knocked about, and we both know there's a lot of stuff talked about—eh, eh, well, you know:—the one and only —that a fellow can't be awfully well smashed by two at the same time don't you know! All rubbish! You know it, and the proof of the puddin's in the eatin', I am!
VIDA. (*As before.*) May I ask where I come in?

SIR WILFRID. Well, now, Mrs. Phillimore, I'll be frank with you, Cynthia's my favorite, but you're runnin' her a close second in the popular esteem!

VIDA. (*Laughs, determined not to take offense.*) What a delightful, original, fantastic person you are!

SIR WILFRID. (*Frankly happy that he has explained everything so neatly.*) I knew you'd take it that way!

VIDA. And what next, pray?

SIR WILFRID. Oh, just the usual,—eh,—thing,—the—eh—the same old question don't you know. Will you have me if she don't?

VIDA. (*A shade piqued, but determined not to risk showing it.*) And you call that the same old usual question?

SIR WILFRID. Yes, I know, but—but will you? I sail in a week; we can take the same boat. And—eh—eh—my dear Mrs.—mayn't I say Vida, I'd like to see you at the head of my table.

VIDA. (*With velvet irony.*) With Cynthia at the foot?

SIR WILFRID. (*Practical, as before.*) Never mind Mrs. Karslake,—I admire her—she's—but you have your own points! And you're here, and so'm I!—damme I offer myself, and my affections, and I'm no icicle, my dear, tell you that for a fact, and, and in fact what's your answer!— (VIDA *sighs and shakes her head.*) Make it, yes! I say, you know, my dear Vida— (*He catches her hands.*)

VIDA. (*She slips them from him.*) Unhand me, dear villain! And sit further away from your second choice! What can I say? I'd rather have *you* for a lover than any man I know! You must be a lovely lover!

SIR WILFRID. I am! (*He makes a second effort to catch her fingers.*)

VIDA. Will you kindly go further away and be good!

SIR WILFRID. (*Quite forgetting* CYNTHIA.) Look here, if you say yes, we'll be married—

VIDA. In a month!

SIR WILFRID. Oh, no—this evening!

VIDA. (*Incapable of leaving a situation unadorned.*) This evening! And sail in the same boat with *you?* And shall we sail to the Garden of Eden and stroll into it and lock the gate on the inside and then lose the key—under a rose-bush?

SIR WILFRID. (*Pauses, and after consideration, says:*) Yes; yes, I say—that's too clever for me! (*He draws nearer to her to bring the understanding to a crisis.*)

VIDA. (*Soft knock up* L.) My maid—come!

SIR WILFRID. (*Swings out of his chair and goes to sofa.*) Eh? (*Enter* BENSON *up* L.)

BENSON. (*To* VIDA.) The new footman, ma'am—he's made a mistake. He's told the lady you're at home.

VIDA. What lady?

BENSON. Mrs. Karslake; and she's on the stairs, ma'am.

VIDA. Show her in.

(SIR WILFRID *has been turning over the roses. On hearing this, he faces about with a long stemmed one in his hand. He uses it in the following scene to point his remarks.*)

SIR WILFRID. (*To* BENSON, *who stops.*) One moment! (*To* VIDA.) I say, eh—I'd rather not see her!

VIDA. (*Very innocently.*) But you came here to see her.

SIR WILFRID. (*A little flustered.*) I'd rather not. Eh,—I fancied I'd find you and her together—but her—(*Comes a step nearer.*) findin' me with you looks so dooced intimate,—no one else, d'ye see, I believe she'd—draw conclusions—

BENSON. Pardon me, ma'am—but I hear Brooks coming!
SIR WILFRID. (*To* BENSON.) Hold the door!
VIDA. So you don't want her to know—?
SIR WILFRID. (*To* VIDA.) Be a good girl now—run me off somewhere!
VIDA. (*To* BENSON.) Show Sir Wilfrid the men's room.

(*Enter* BROOKS, L.)

SIR WILFRID. The men's room! Ah! Oh! Eh!
VIDA. (*Beckons him to go at once.*) Sir Wil— (*He hesitates, then as* BROOKS *comes on, he flings off with* BENSON.)
BROOKS. Lady Karslake, milady!
VIDA. Anything more inopportune! I never dreamed she'd come— (*Enter* CYNTHIA, *veiled. She comes down quickly. Langourously.*) My dear Cynthia, you don't mean to say—
CYNTHIA. (*Rather short, and visibly agitated.*) Yes, I've come.
VIDA. (*Polite, but not urgent.*) Do take off your veil.
CYNTHIA. (*Doing as* VIDA *asks.*) Is no one here?
VIDA. (*As before.*) Won't you sit down?
CYNTHIA. (*Agitated and suspicious.*) Thanks, no— That is, yes, thanks. Yes! You haven't answered my question? (CYNTHIA *waves her hand through the smoke, looks at the smoke suspiciously, looks for the cigarette.*)
VIDA. (*Playing innocence in the first degree.*) My dear, what makes you imagine that any one's here!
CYNTHIA. You've been smoking.
VIDA. Oh, puffing away! (CYNTHIA *sees the glasses up* R.)
CYNTHIA. And drinking—a pair of drinks? (*She sees* JOHN'S *gloves on the table at her elbow.*) Do they fit you, dear? (VIDA *smiles;* CYNTHIA *picks up crop and*

looks at it and reads her own name.) "Jack, from Cynthia."

VIDA. (*Assured, and without taking the trouble to double for a mere woman.*) Yes, dear; it's Mr. Karslake's crop, but I'm happy to say he left me a few minutes ago.

CYNTHIA. He left the house? (VIDA *smiles.*) I wanted to see him.

VIDA. (*With a shade of insolence.*) To quarrel?

CYNTHIA. (*Frank and curt.*) I wanted to see him.

VIDA. (*Determined to put* CYNTHIA *in the wrong.*) And I sent him away because I didn't want you to repeat the scene of last night in my house.

CYNTHIA. (*Looks at crop and is silent.*) Well, I can't stay. I'm to be married at three, and I had to play truant to get here!

(*Enter* BENSON, *up* L.)

BENSON. (*To* VIDA.) There's a person, ma'am, on the sidewalk.

VIDA. What person, Benson?

BENSON. A person, ma'am, with a horse.

CYNTHIA. (*Happily agitated.*) It's Fiddler with Cynthia K! (*She goes up rapidly and looks out back through window.*)

VIDA. (*To* BENSON.) Tell the man I'll be down in five minutes.

CYNTHIA. (*Looking down from the balcony with delight.*) Oh, there she is!

VIDA. (*Aside to* BENSON.) Go to the club room, Benson, and say to the two gentlemen I can't see them at present—I'll send for them when—

BENSON. (*Listens* L.) I hear some one coming.

VIDA. Quick!

(BENSON *crosses* L. *Door* L. *opens, and* JOHN *enters.* JOHN *comes in slowly, carelessly.* VIDA *whispers to* BENSON.)

BENSON. (*Crosses, goes close to* JOHN *and whispers.*) Beg par—

VIDA. (*Under her breath.*) Go back!

JOHN. (*Not understanding.*) I beg pardon!

VIDA. (*As before.*) Go back!

JOHN. (*The same.*) Can't! I've a date! With the sheriff!

VIDA. (*A little cross.*) Please use your eyes.

JOHN. (*Laughing and flattering* VIDA.) I am using my eyes.

VIDA. (*Fretted.*) Don't you see there's a lovely creature in the room?

JOHN. (*Again taking the loud upperhand.*) Of course there is.

VIDA. Hush!

JOHN. (*Teasingly.*) But what I want to know is—

VIDA. Hush!

JOHN. (*Delighted at getting a rise.*) —is when we're to stroll in the Garden of Eden—

VIDA. Hush!

JOHN. —and lose the key. (*To put a stop to this, she lightly tosses her handkerchief into his face.*) By George, talk about attar of roses!

CYNTHIA. (*Up at window, excited and moved at seeing her mare once more.*) Oh, she's a darling! (*She turns.*) A perfect darling! (JOHN *starts up; sees* CYNTHIA *at the same instant that she sees him.*) Oh! I didn't know you were here. (*Pause; then with "take-it-or-leave-it" frankness.*) I came to see *you!* (JOHN *looks extremely dark and angry;* VIDA *rises.*)

VIDA. (*To* CYNTHIA, *most gently, and seeing there's nothing to be made of* JOHN.) Oh, pray feel at home, Cynthia, dear! (*Stands by door,* R.; *to* JOHN.) When I've a nice street frock on, I'll ask you to present me to Cynthia K. (*Exit* VIDA, R. JOHN *and* CYNTHIA, *tableau.*)

CYNTHIA. (*Agitated and frank.*) Of course, I told you yesterday I was coming here.

JOHN. (R., *irritated.*) And I was to deny myself the privilege of being here?

CYNTHIA. (*Curt and agitated.*) Yes.

JOHN. (*Ready to fight.*) And you guessed I would do that?

CYNTHIA. No.

JOHN. What?

CYNTHIA. (*Above table. She speaks with agitation, frankness and good will.*) Jack—I mean, Mr. Karslake, —no, I mean, Jack! I came because—well, you see, it's my wedding day!—and—and—I—I—was rude to you last evening. I'd like to apologize and make peace with you before I go—

JOHN. (*Determined to be disagreeable.*) Before you go to your last, long home!

CYNTHIA. I came to apologize.

JOHN. But you'll remain to quarrel!

CYNTHIA. (*Still frank and kind.*) I will not quarrel. No!—and I'm only here for a moment. I'm to be married at three, and just look at the clock! Besides, I told Philip I was going to Louise's shop, and I did—on the way here; but, you see, if I stay too long he'll telephone Louise and find I'm not there, and he might guess I was here. So you see I'm risking a scandal. And now, Jack, see here, I lay my hand on the table, I'm here on the square, and,—what I want to say is, why—Jack, even if we have made a mess of our married life, let's put by anger and pride. It's all over now and can't be helped. So let's be human, let's be reasonable, and let's be kind to each other! Won't you give me your hand? (JOHN *refuses*, R.) I wish you every happiness!

JOHN. (*Turns away* R., *the past rankling.*) I had a client once, a murderer; he told me he murdered the man, and he told me, too, that he never felt so kindly to anybody as he did to that man after he'd killed him!

CYNTHIA. Jack!

JOHN. (*Unforgiving.*) You murdered my happiness!
CYNTHIA. I won't recriminate!
JOHN. And now I must put by anger and pride! I do! But not self-respect, not a just indignation—not the facts and my clear memory of them!
CYNTHIA. Jack!
JOHN. No!
CYNTHIA. (*Goes c., with growing emotion, and holds out her hand.*) I give you one more chance! Yes, I'm determined to be generous. I forgive everything you ever did to me. I'm ready to be friends. I wish you every happiness and every—every—horse in the world! I can't do more than that! (*She offers it again.*) You refuse?
JOHN. (*Moved but surly.*) I like wildcats and I like Christians, but I don't like Christian wildcats! Now I'm close hauled, trot out your tornado! Let the Tiger loose! It's the tamer, the man in the cage that has to look lively and use the red hot crowbar! But by Jove, I'm out of the cage! I'm a mere spectator of the married circus! (*He puffs vigorously.*)
CYNTHIA. Be a game sport then! Our marriage was a wager; you wagered you could live with me. You lost; you paid with a divorce; and now is the time to show your sporting blood. Come on, shake hands and part friends.
JOHN. Not in this world! Friends with you, no! I have a proper pride. I don't propose to put my pride in my pocket.
CYNTHIA. (*Jealous and plain spoken.*) Oh, I wouldn't ask you to put your pride in your pocket while Vida's handkerchief is there. (JOHN *looks angered.*) Pretty little bijou of a handkerchief! (CYNTHIA *takes handkerchief out.*) And she is charming, and divorced, and reasonably well made up.
JOHN. Oh, well, Vida is a woman. (*Business with*

handkerchief.) I'm a man, a handkerchief is a handkerchief, and as some old Aristotle or other said, whatever concerns a woman, concerns me!

CYNTHIA. (*Not oblivious of him, but in a low voice.*) Insufferable! Well, yes. (*She sits. She is too much wounded to make any further appeal.*) You're perfectly right. There's no possible harmony between divorced people! I withdraw my hand and all good feeling. No wonder I couldn't stand you. Eh? However, that's pleasantly past! But at least, my dear Karslake, let us have some sort of beauty of behavior! If we cannot be decent, let us endeavor to be graceful. If we can't be moral, at least we can avoid being vulgar.

JOHN. Well—

CYNTHIA. If there's to be no more marriage in the world—

JOHN. (*Cynical.*) Oh, but that's not it; there's to be more and more and more!

CYNTHIA. (*With a touch of bitterness.*) Very well! I repeat then, if there's to be nothing but marriage and divorce, and remarriage, and redivorce, at least, at least, those who *are* divorced can avoid the vulgarity of meeting each other here, there, and everywhere!

JOHN. Oh, that's where you come out!

CYNTHIA. I thought so yesterday, and to-day I know it. It's an insufferable thing to a woman of any delicacy of feeling to find her husband—

JOHN. Ahem—former!

CYNTHIA. *Once* a husband always—

JOHN. (*Still cynical.*) Oh, no! Oh, dear, no.

CYNTHIA. To find her—to find the man she has once lived with—in the house of—making love to—to find you here! (JOHN *smiles; rises.*) You smile,—but I say, it should be a social axiom, no woman should have to meet her former husband.

JOHN. (*Cynical and cutting.*) Oh, I don't know; after I've served my term I don't mind meeting my jailor.

CYNTHIA. (JOHN *takes chair near* CYNTHIA.) It's indecent—at the horse-show, the opera, at races and balls, to meet the man who once—It's not civilized! It's fantastic! It's half baked! Oh, I never should have come here! (*He sympathizes, and she grows irrational and furious.*) But it's entirely your fault!

JOHN. My fault?

CYNTHIA. (*Working herself into a rage.*) Of course. What business have you to be about—to be at large. To be at all!

JOHN. Gosh!

CYNTHIA. (*As before.*) To be where I am! Yes, it's just as horrible for you to turn up in my life as it would be for a dead person to insist on coming back to life and dinner and bridge!

JOHN. Horrid idea!

CYNTHIA. Yes, but it's *you* who behave just as if you were not dead, just as if I'd not spent a fortune on your funeral. You do; you prepare to bob up at afternoon teas,—and dinners—and embarrass me to death with your extinct personality!

JOHN. Well, of course we *were* married, but it didn't quite kill me.

CYNTHIA. (*Angry and plain spoken.*) You killed yourself for me—I divorced you. I buried you out of my life. If any human soul was ever dead, you are! And there's nothing I so hate as a gibbering ghost.

JOHN. Oh, I say!

CYNTHIA. (*With hot anger.*) Go gibber and squeak where gibbering and squeaking are the fashion!

JOHN. (*Laughs, pretending to a coldness he does not feel.*) And so, my dear child, I'm to abate myself as a nuisance! Well, as far as seeing you is concerned, for my part it's just like seeing a horse who's chucked you once.

The bruises are O.K., and you see him with a sort of easy curiosity. Of course, you know, he'll jolly well chuck the next man!—Permit me! (JOHN *picks up gloves, handkerchief and parasol and gives her these as she drops them one by one in her agitation.*) There's pleasure in the thought.

CYNTHIA. Oh!

JOHN. And now, may I ask you a very simple question? Mere curiosity on my part, but, why did you come here this morning?

CYNTHIA. I have already explained that to you.

JOHN. Not your real motive. Permit me!

CYNTHIA. Oh!

JOHN. But I believe I have guessed your real—permit me—your real motive!

CYNTHIA. Oh!

JOHN. (*With mock sympathy.*) Cynthia, I am sorry for you.

CYNTHIA. Hm?

JOHN. Of course we had a pretty lively case of the fever—the mutual attraction fever, and we *were* married a very short time. And I conclude that's what's the matter with *you!* You see, my dear, seven months of married life is too short a time to cure a bad case of the fancies.

CYNTHIA. (*In angry surprise.*) What?

JOHN. (*Calm and triumphant.*) That's my diagnosis.

CYNTHIA. (*Simply and gathering herself together.*) I don't think I understand.

JOHN. Oh, yes, you do; yes, you do.

CYNTHIA. (*With blazing eyes.*) What do you mean?

JOHN. Would you mind not breaking my crop! Thank you! I mean (*With polite impertinence.*) that ours was a case of premature divorce, and, ahem, you're in love with me still. (*Pause.* CYNTHIA *has one moment of fury, then she realizes at what a disadvantage this places her. She makes an immense effort, recovers her calm, thinks hard for a moment more, and then, has suddenly an inspiration.*)

CYNTHIA. Jack, some day you'll get the blind staggers from conceit. No, I'm not in love with you, Mr. Karslake, but I shouldn't be at all surprised if she were. She's just your sort, you know. She's a man-eating shark, and you'll be a toothsome mouthful. Oh, come now, Jack, what a silly you are! Oh, yes, you are, to get off a joke like that; me—in love with— (*Looks at him.*)

JOHN. Why are you here? (*She laughs and begins to play her game.*) Why are you here?

CYNTHIA. Guess! (*She laughs.*)

JOHN. Why are you—

CYNTHIA. (*Quickly.*) Why am I here! I'll tell you. I'm going to be married. I had a longing, an irresistible longing to see you make an ass of yourself just once more! It happened!

JOHN. (*Uncertain and discomfited.*) I know better!

CYNTHIA. But I came for a serious purpose, too. I came, my dear fellow, to make an experiment on myself. I've been with you thirty minutes; and— (*She sighs with content.*) It's all right!

JOHN. What's all right?

CYNTHIA. (*Calm and apparently at peace with the world.*) I'm immune.

JOHN. Immune?

CYNTHIA. You're not catching any more! Yes, you see, I said to myself, if I fly into a temper—

JOHN. You did!

CYNTHIA. If I fly into a temper when I see him, well that shows I'm not yet so entirely convalescent that I can afford to have Jack Karslake at my house. If I remain calm I shall ask him to dinner.

JOHN. (*Routed.*) Ask me if you dare! (*Rises.*)

CYNTHIA. (*Getting the whip hand for good.*) Ask you to dinner? Oh, my dear fellow. (JOHN *rises.*) I'm going to

ACT II   THE NEW YORK IDEA   69

do much more than that. (*Rises.*) We must be friends, old man! We must meet, we must meet often, we must show New York the way the thing should be done, and, to show you I mean it— I want you to be my best man, and give me away when I'm married this afternoon.

JOHN. (*Incredulous and impatient.*) You don't mean that! (*Puts back chair.*)

CYNTHIA. There you are! Always suspicious!

JOHN. You don't mean that!

CYNTHIA. (*Hiding her emotion under a sportswoman's manner.*) Don't I? I ask you, come! And come as you are! And I'll lay my wedding gown to Cynthia K that you won't be there! If you're there, you get the gown, and if you're not, I get Cynthia K!—

JOHN. (*Determined not to be worsted.*) I take it!

CYNTHIA. Done! Now, then, we'll see which of us two is the real sporting goods! Shake! (*They shake hands on it.*) Would you mind letting me have a plain soda? (JOHN *goes to the table, as he is rattled and does not regard what he is about, he fills the glass three-fourths full with whiskey. He comes to* CYNTHIA *and gives her this. She looks him in the eye with an air of triumph.*) Thanks. (*Maliciously, as* VIDA *enters.*) Your hand is a bit shaky. I think *you* need a little King William. (JOHN *shrugs his shoulders, and as* VIDA *immediately speaks,* CYNTHIA *defers drinking.*)

VIDA (*To* CYNTHIA.) My dear, I'm sorry to tell you your husband—I mean, my husband—I mean Philip— he's asking for you over the 'phone. You must have said you were coming here. Of course, I told him you were not here, and hung up.

(*Enter* BENSON.)

BENSON. (*To* VIDA.) Ma'am, the new footman's been talking with Mr. Phillimore on the wire. (VIDA, *gesture of regret.*) He told Mr. Phillimore that his lady was here, and if I can believe my ears, ma'am, he's got Sir Wilfrid on the 'phone now!

(*Enter* SIR WILFRID.)

SIR WILFRID. (*Comes from* L., *perplexed and annoyed.*) I say y' know—extraordinary country; that old chap, Phillimore, he's been damned impertinent over the wire! Says I've run off with Mrs. Karslake—talks about "Louise!" Now who the dooce is Louise? He's comin' round here, too—I said Mrs. Karslake wasn't here— (*Sees* CYNTHIA.) Hello! Good job! What a liar I am!

BENSON. (*To* VIDA.) Mr. Fiddler, ma'am, says the mare is gettin' very restive. (*Comes up to door.* JOHN *hears this and moves at once. Exit* BENSON.)

JOHN. (*To* VIDA.) If that mare's restive, she'll break out in a rash.

VIDA. (*To* JOHN.) Will you take me?

JOHN. Of course. (*They go up to exit* L.)

CYNTHIA. (*To* JOHN.) Tata, old man! Meet you at the altar! If I don't the mare's mine! (SIR WILFRID *looks at her amazed.*)

VIDA. (*To* CYNTHIA.) Do the honors, dear, in my absence!

JOHN. Come along, come along, never mind them! A horse is a horse!

(*Exeunt* JOHN *and* VIDA, L., *gaily and in haste. At the same moment* CYNTHIA *drinks what she supposes to be her glass of plain soda. As it is whiskey straight, she is seized with astonishment and a fit of coughing.* SIR WILFRID *relieves her of the glass.*)

SIR WILFRID. (*Indicating contents of glass.*) I say, do you ordinarily take it as high up—as seven fingers and two thumbs.

ACT II THE NEW YORK IDEA 71

CYNTHIA. (*Coughs.*) Jack poured it out. Just shows how groggy he was! And now, Sir Wilfrid— (*Gets her things to go.*)

SIR WILFRID. Oh, you can't go!

(*Enter* BROOKS.)

CYNTHIA. I am to be married at three.

SIR WILFRID. Let him wait. (*To* BROOKS, *whom he meets near the door; aside.*) If Mr. Phillimore comes, bring his card up.

BROOKS. (*Going.*) Yes, Sir Wilfrid.

SIR WILFRID. (*To* BROOKS, *as before.*) To me! (*He tips him.*)

BROOKS. (*Bowing.*) To you, Sir Wilfrid. (*Exit* BROOKS.)

SIR WILFRID. (*Returning to* CYNTHIA.) I've got to have my innings, y' know! (*He looks at her more closely.*) I say, you've been crying!—

CYNTHIA. King William!

SIR WILFRID. You *are* crying! Poor little gal!

CYNTHIA. (*Tears in her eyes.*) I feel all shaken and cold.

(*Enter* BROOKS, *with card.*)

SIR WILFRID. (*Astonished and sympathetic.*) Poor little gal.

CYNTHIA. (*As before.*) I didn't sleep a wink last night. (*With disgust.*) Oh, what is the matter with me?

SIR WILFRID. Why, it's as plain as a pikestaff! You— (BROOKS *has brought salver to* SIR WILFRID. *A card lies upon it.* SIR WILFRID *takes it and says aside to* BROOKS.) Phillimore? (BROOKS *assents. Aloud to* CYNTHIA, *calmly deceitful.*) Who's Waldorf Smith? (CYNTHIA *shakes her head. To* BROOKS, *returning card to salver.*) Tell the gentleman Mrs. Karslake is not here! (*Exit* BROOKS.)

CYNTHIA. (*Aware that she has no business where she is.*) I thought it was Philip!

SIR WILFRID. (*Telling the truth as if it were a lie.*) So did I! (*With cheerful confidence.*) And now, Mrs. Karslake, I'll tell you why you're cryin'. (*He sits beside her.*) You're marryin' the wrong man! I'm sorry for you, but you're such a goose. Here you are, marryin' this legal luminary. What for? You don't know! He don't know! But I do! You pretend you're marryin' him because it's the sensible thing; not a bit of it. You're marryin' Mr. Phillimore because of all the other men you ever saw he's the least like Jack Karslake.

CYNTHIA. That's a very good reason.

SIR WILFRID. There's only one good reason for marrying, and that is because you'll die if you don't!

CYNTHIA. Oh, I've tried that!

SIR WILFRID. The Scripture says: "Try! try! again!" I tell you, there's nothing like a w'im!

CYNTHIA. What's that? W'im? Oh, you mean a *whim!* Do please try and say W*h*im!

SIR WILFRID. (*For the first time emphasizing his H in the word.*) W*h*im. You must have a w'im—w'im for the chappie you marry.

CYNTHIA. I had—for Jack.

SIR WILFRID. Your w'im wasn't wimmy enough, my dear! If you'd had more of it, and tougher, it would ha' stood y' know! Now, I'm not proposin'!

CYNTHIA. (*Diverted at last from her own distress.*) I hope not!

SIR WILFRID. Oh, I will later! It's not time yet! As I was saying—

CYNTHIA. And pray, Sir Wilfrid, when will it be time?

SIR WILFRID. As soon as I see you have a w'im for me!

ACT II   THE NEW YORK IDEA   73

(*Rising, looks at his watch.*) And now, I'll tell you what we'll do! We've got just an hour to get there in, my motor's on the corner, and in fifty minutes we'll be at Belmont Park.

CYNTHIA. (*Her sporting blood fired.*) Belmont Park!

SIR WILFRID. We'll do the races, and dine at Martin's—

CYNTHIA. (*Tempted.*) Oh, if I only could! I can't! I've got to be married! You're awfully nice; I've almost got a "w'im" for you already.

SIR WILFRID. (*Delighted.*) There you are! I'll send a telegram! (*She shakes her head. He sits and writes at the table,* L.)

CYNTHIA. No, no, no!

SIR WILFRID. (*Reads what he writes.*) "Off with Cates-Darby to Races. Please postpone ceremony till seven-thirty."

CYNTHIA. Oh, no, it's impossible!

SIR WILFRID. (*Accustomed to have things go his way.*) No more than breathin'! You can't get a w'im for me, you know, unless we're together, so together we'll be! (*Enter* JOHN KARSLAKE.) And to-morrow you'll wake up with a jolly little w'im— (*Reads.*) "Postpone ceremony till seven-thirty." There. (*He puts on her cloak. Sees* JOHN.) Hello!

JOHN. (*Surly.*) Hello! Sorry to disturb you.

SIR WILFRID. (*Cheerful as possible.*) Just the man! (*Gives him the telegraph form.*) Just step round and send it, my boy. Thanks! (JOHN *reads it.*)

CYNTHIA. No, no, I can't go!

SIR WILFRID. Cockety-coo-coo-can't. I say, you must!

CYNTHIA. (*Positively.*) *No!*

JOHN. (*Astounded.*) Do you mean you're going—

SIR WILFRID. (*Very gay.*) Off to the races, my boy!

JOHN. (*Angry and outraged.*) Mrs. Karslake can't go with you there!

(CYNTHIA *starts, amazed at his assumption of marital authority, and delighted that she will have an opportunity of outraging his sensibilities.*)

SIR WILFRID. Oho!

JOHN. An hour before her wedding!

SIR WILFRID. (*Gay and not angry.*) May I know if it's the custom—

JOHN. (*Jealous and disgusted.*) It's worse than eloping—

SIR WILFRID. Custom, y' know, for the husband, that was, to dictate—

JOHN. (*Thoroughly vexed.*) By George, there's a limit!

CYNTHIA. What? What? What? (*Gathers up her things.*) What did I hear you say?

SIR WILFRID. Aha!

JOHN. (*Angry.*) I say there's a limit—

CYNTHIA. (*More and more determined to arouse and excite* JOHN.) Oh, there's a limit, is there?

JOHN. There is! I bar the way! It means reputation— it means—

CYNTHIA. (*Enjoying her opportunity.*) We shall see what it means!

SIR WILFRID. Aha!

JOHN. (*To* CYNTHIA.) I'm here to protect your reputation—

SIR WILFRID. (*To* CYNTHIA.) We've got to make haste, you know.

CYNTHIA. Now, I'm ready—

JOHN. (*To* CYNTHIA.) Be sensible. You're breaking off the match—

ACT II THE NEW YORK IDEA 75

CYNTHIA. (*Excitedly.*) What's that to you?

SIR WILFRID. It's boots and saddles!

JOHN. (*He takes his stand between them and the door.*) No thoroughfare!

SIR WILFRID. Look here, my boy—!

CYNTHIA. (*Catching at the opportunity of putting* JOHN *in an impossible position.*) Wait a moment, Sir Wilfrid! Give me the wire! (*Faces him.*) Thanks! (*She takes the telegraph form from him and tears it up.*) There! Too rude to chuck him by wire! But you, Jack, you've taken on yourself to look after my interests, so I'll just ask you, old man, to run down to the Supreme Court and tell Philip—nicely, you know—I'm off with Sir Wilfrid and where! Say I'll be back by seven, if I'm not later! And make it clear, Jack, I'll marry him by eight-thirty or nine at the latest! And mind *you're* there, dear! And now, Sir Wilfrid, we're off.

JOHN. (*Staggered and furious, giving way as they pass him.*) I'm not the man to—to carry—

CYNTHIA. (*Quick and dashing.*) Oh, yes, you are.

JOHN. —a message from you.

CYNTHIA. (*Triumphant.*) Oh, yes, you are; you're just exactly the man! (*Exeunt* CYNTHIA *and* SIR WILFRID.)

JOHN. Great miracles of Moses!

CURTAIN

ACT THREE

SCENE: *The same as that of Act I, but the room has been cleared of too much furniture, and arranged for a wedding ceremony. The curtain rises on* MRS. PHILLIMORE *reclining on the sofa,* L. MISS HENEAGE *is seated left of table,* R. SUDLEY *is seated at the right of the table.* GRACE *is seated on sofa,* L. *There are cushions of flowers, alcove of flowers, flowers in vase, pink and white hangings, wedding bell of roses, calla lilies, orange blossoms, a ribbon of white stretched in front of an altar of flowers; two cushions for the couple to kneel on; two candelabra at each side of back of arch on pedestals.*

(*The curtain rises. There is a momentary silence, that the audience may take in these symbols of marriage, etc. Every member of the Phillimore family is irritable, with suppressed irritation.*

SUDLEY. (*Impatiently.*) All very well, my dear Sarah. But you see the hour. Twenty to ten! We have been here since half-past two.

MISS HENEAGE. You had dinner?

SUDLEY. I did not come here at two to have dinner at eight, and be kept waiting until ten! And, my dear Sarah, when I ask where the bride is—

MISS HENEAGE. (*With forced composure.*) I have told you all I know. Mr. John Karslake came to the house at lunch time, spoke to Philip, and they left the house together.

GRACE. Where is Philip?

MRS. PHILLIMORE. (*Feebly, irritated.*) I don't wish to

be censorious or to express an actual opinion, but I must say it's a bold bride who keeps her future mother-in-law waiting for eight hours. However, I will not venture to— (MRS. PHILLIMORE *reclines again and fades away into silence.*)

GRACE. (*Sharply and decisively.*) I do! I'm sorry I went to the expense of a silver ice-pitcher. (MRS. PHILLIMORE *sighs.* MISS HENEAGE *keeps her temper with an effort which is obvious. Enter* THOMAS.)

SUDLEY. (*To* MRS. PHILLIMORE.) For my part, I don't believe Mrs. Karslake means to return here or to marry Philip at all!

THOMAS. (R. C., *to* MISS HENEAGE.) Two telegrams for you, ma'am! The choir boys have had their supper. (*Slight movement from every one;* THOMAS *steps back.*)

SUDLEY. (*Rises.*) At last we shall know!

MISS HENEAGE. From the lady! Probably! (MISS HENEAGE *opens telegram; reads first one at a glance, lays it on salver again with a glance at* SUDLEY. THOMAS *passes salver to* SUDLEY, *who takes telegram.*)

GRACE. There's a toot now.

MRS. PHILLIMORE. (*Feebly, confused.*) I don't wish to intrude, but really I cannot imagine Philip marrying at midnight.

(*As* SUDLEY *reads,* MISS HENEAGE *opens the second telegram, but does not read it.*)

SUDLEY. (*Reads.*) "Accident, auto struck"—something! "Gasoline"—did something—illegible, ah! (*Reads.*) "Home by nine forty-five! Hold the church!" (*General movement from all.*)

MISS HENEAGE. (*Profoundly shocked.*) "Hold the church!" William, she still means to marry Philip! and to-night, too!

Sudley. It's from Belmont Park.

Grace. (*Making a great discovery.*) She went to the races!

Miss Heneage. This is from Philip! (Miss Heneage *reads second telegram.*) "I arrive at ten o'clock. Have dinner ready." (Miss Heneage *motions to* Thomas *to withdraw.* Thomas *exits,* L. Miss Heneage *looks at her watch.*) They are both due now. (*Movement.*) What's to be done? (*Rises.* Sudley *shrugs shoulders.*)

Sudley. (*Rises.*) After a young woman has spent her wedding day at the races? Why, I consider that she has broken the engagement,—and when she comes, tell her so.

Miss Heneage. I'll telephone Matthew. The choir boys can go home—her maid can pack her belongings—and when the lady arrives—

(*Very distant toot of an auto-horn is heard. Tableau. Auto-horn a little louder.* Grace *flies up stage and looks out of door* R. Mrs. Phillimore *does not know what to do, or where to go.* Sudley *crosses* R., *excitedly.* Miss Heneage *stands ready to make herself disagreeable.*)

Grace. (*Speaking rapidly and with excitement.*) I hear a man's voice. Cates-Darby and brother Matthew.

(*Loud toot. Laughter and voices off back, faintly.* Grace *looks out of door, and then comes rapidly down* L.)

Miss Heneage. Outrageous!

Sudley. Disgraceful!

Mrs. Phillimore. Shocking! (*Voices and horn off; a little louder. Partly rising.*) I shall not take any part at all, in the—eh— (*She fades away.*)

Miss Heneage. (*Interrupting her.*) Don't trouble yourself.

(*Voices and laughter, louder.* Cynthia's *voice is heard off.* Sir Wilfrid *appears back. He turns and waits for* Cynthia *and* Matthew. *He carries wraps. He speaks to* Cynthia, *who is still off.* Matthew's *voice is heard and* Cynthia's. Cynthia *appears at back, followed by* Matthew. *As they appear,* Cynthia *speaks to* Matthew, *on her right.* Sir Wilfrid *carries a newspaper and parasol. The hat is the one she wore in Act II. She is in getup for auto. Goggles, veil, an exquisite duster in latest Paris style. All three come down rapidly. As she appears,* Sudley *and* Miss Heneage *exclaim, and there is a general movement.*)

Sudley. (*To table,* L.) 'Pon my word!
Grace. Hah!
Miss Heneage. (*Rises,* R.) Shocking!

(Grace *remains standing above sofa.* Sudley *moves toward her.* Miss Heneage *sits.* Mrs. Phillimore *reclines on sofa* L. Cynthia *begins to speak as soon as she apears and speaks fluently to the end.*)

Cynthia. (C.) No! I never was so surprised in my life, as when I strolled into the paddock and they gave me a rousing reception—old Jimmy Withers, Debt Gollup, Jack Deal, Monty Spiffles, the Governor and Buckeye. All of my old admirers! They simply fell on my neck, and dear Matthew, what do you think I did? I turned on the water main! (*Movements and murmurs of disapprobation from the family.* Matthew *indicates a desire to go.*) Oh, but you can't go!

MATTHEW. I'll return in no time!

CYNTHIA. I'm all ready to be married. Are they ready? (MATTHEW *waves a pious, polite gesture of recognition to the family.*) I beg everybody's pardon! (*She takes off her wrap and puts it on the back of a chair up stage.*) My goggles are so dusty, I can't see who's who! (*To* SIR WILFRID.) Thanks! You *have* carried it well!

(*Parasol from* SIR WILFRID.)

SIR WILFRID. (*Aside to* CYNTHIA.) When may I—?

CYNTHIA. See you next Goodwood!

SIR WILFRID. (*Imperturbably.*) Oh, I'm coming back! (CYNTHIA *comes down.*)

CYNTHIA. Not a bit of use in coming back! I shall be married before you get here! Ta! Ta! Goodwood!

SIR WILFRID. (*As before.*) I'm coming back. (*He goes out* L., *quickly. More murmurs of disapprobation from family. Slight pause.*)

CYNTHIA. (*Begins to take off her goggles, and comes down slowly.*) I do awfully apologize for being so late!

MISS HENEAGE. (*Importantly.*) Mrs. Karslake—

SUDLEY. (*Importantly.*) Ahem! (CYNTHIA *lays down goggles, and sees their severity.*)

CYNTHIA. Dear me! (*She surveys the flowers, and for a moment pauses.*) Oh, good heavens! Why, it looks like a smart funeral! (MISS HENEAGE *moves; then speaks in a perfectly ordinary natural tone, but her expression is severe.* CYNTHIA *immediately realizes the state of affairs in its fullness.*)

MISS HENEAGE. (*To* CYNTHIA.) After what has occurred, Mrs. Karslake— (CYNTHIA *glances at table* L.)

CYNTHIA. (*Sits* R. *of table, composed and good tempered.*) I see you got my wire—so you know where I have been.

MISS HENEAGE. To the race-course!

SUDLEY. (*Goes up to* C.) With a rowdy Englishman,

(CYNTHIA *glances at* SUDLEY, *uncertain whether he means to be disagreeable, or whether he is only naturally so.*)

MISS HENEAGE. We concluded you desired to break the engagement!

CYNTHIA. (*Indifferently.*) No! No! Oh! No!

MISS HENEAGE. Do you intend, despite of our opinion of you—

CYNTHIA. The only opinion that would have any weight with me would be Mrs. Phillimore's. (*She turns expectantly to* MRS. PHILLIMORE.)

MRS. PHILLIMORE. I am generally asleep at this hour, and accordingly I will not venture to express any—eh— any—actual opinion. (*Fades away.* CYNTHIA *smiles.*)

MISS HENEAGE. (*Coldly.*) You smile. We simply inform you that as regards *us*, the alliance is not grateful.

CYNTHIA. (*Affecting gaiety and unconcern.*) And all this because the gasoline gave out.

SUDLEY. My patience has given out!

GRACE. So has mine. I'm going. (*Exit* GRACE.)

SUDLEY. (*Comes down* C., *vexed beyond civility. To* CYNTHIA.) My dear young lady: You come here, to this sacred—eh—eh—spot—altar!— (*Gesture.*) odoriferous of the paddock!—speaking of Spiffles and Buckeye, —having practically eloped!—having created a scandal, and disgraced our family!

CYNTHIA. (*As before.*) How does it disgrace you? Because I like to see a high-bred, clean, nervy, sweet little four-legged gee play the antelope over a hurdle!

MISS HENEAGE. Sister, it is high time that you— (*Turns to* CYNTHIA. *Gesture.*)

CYNTHIA. (*With quiet irony.*) Mrs. Phillimore is generally asleep at this hour, and accordingly she will not venture to express—

SUDLEY. (*Spluttering with irritation.*) Enough, madam

—I *venture* to—to—to—to say, you are leading a fast life.

CYNTHIA. (*With powerful intention.*) Not in this house! For six heavy weeks have I been laid away in the grave, and I've found it very slow indeed trying to keep pace with the dead!

SUDLEY. (*Despairingly.*) This comes of horses!

CYNTHIA. (*Indignant.*) Of what?

SUDLEY. C-c-caring for horses!

MISS HENEAGE. (*With sublime morality.*) What Mrs. Karslake cares for is—men.

CYNTHIA. (*Angry and gay.*) What would you have me care for? The Ornithorhyncus Paradoxus? or Pithacanthropus Erectus? Oh, I refuse to take you seriously. (SUDLEY *begins to prepare to leave; he buttons himself into respectability and his coat.*)

SUDLEY. My dear madam, I take myself seriously— and madam, I—I retract what I have brought with me (*He feels in his waistcoat pocket.*) as a graceful gift,—an Egyptian scarab—a—a—sacred beetle, which once ornamented the person of a—eh—mummy.

CYNTHIA. (*Getting even with him.*) It should never be absent from your pocket, Mr. Sudley! (SUDLEY *goes up in a rage.*)

MISS HENEAGE. (*Rises. To* SUDLEY.) I've a vast mind to withdraw my— (CYNTHIA *moves.*)

CYNTHIA. (*Interrupts; maliciously.*) Your wedding present? The little bronze cat!

MISS HENEAGE. (*Moves, angrily.*) Oh! (*Even* MRS. PHILLIMORE *comes momentarily to life, and expresses silent indignation.*)

SUDLEY. (*Loftily.*) Sarah, I'm going. (*Enter* PHILIP *at back with* GRACE. PHILIP *looks dusty and grim.* GRACE, *as they come in, speaks to him.* PHILIP *shakes his head. They pause up stage.*)

CYNTHIA. (*Emotionally.*) I shall go to my room! (*Goes to* R. SUDLEY *down* L.; MISS HENEAGE, C.; MRS. PHILLIMORE *sees* PHILIP. PHILIP *represses* GRACE; *gives her a stern look and forceful gesture to be silent.* CYNTHIA *goes up, and* MISS HENEAGE *comes down* R.) However, all I ask is that you repeat to Philip— (*Comes suddenly on* PHILIP, *and speaks to him in a low tone.*)

SUDLEY. (*To* MISS HENEAGE, *determined to win.*) As I go out, I shall do myself the pleasure of calling a hansom for Mrs. Karslake— (PHILIP *comes down two or three steps.*)

PHILIP. As you go out, Sudley, have a hansom called, and when it comes, get into it.

SUDLEY. (*Furious, and speaking to* PHILIP.) Eh,—eh, —my dear sir, I leave you to your fate. (PHILIP *angrily points him the door. Exit,* L.)

MISS HENEAGE. (*With weight.*) Philip, you've not heard—

PHILIP. (*Interrupts.*) Everything—from Grace! (CYNTHIA *goes down* R. *of table.*) My sister has repeated your words to me—and her own! I've told her what I think of her. (PHILIP *looks witheringly at* GRACE.)

GRACE. I shan't wait to hear any more. (*Exit* GRACE, *indignantly.*)

PHILIP. Don't make it necessary for me to tell you what I think of you. (PHILIP *crosses* L.; MISS HENEAGE *crosses to* R. *in fury.* PHILIP *gives his arm to his mother.* MISS HENEAGE *goes to door* R.) Mother, with your permission, I desire to be alone. I expect both you and Grace, Sarah, to be dressed and ready for the ceremony a half hour from now. (*As* PHILIP *and* MRS. PHILLIMORE *are about to cross,* MISS HENEAGE *speaks.*)

MISS HENEAGE. (*Up* R.) I shall come or not as I see fit. And let me add, my dear brother, that a fool at forty is a fool indeed. (*Exit* MISS HENEAGE, R., *high and mighty, and much pleased with her quotation.*)

MRS. PHILLIMORE. (*Stupid and weary as usual, to* PHILIP, *as he leads her to the door,* R.) My dear son— I won't venture to express— (CYNTHIA *crosses* L. *to table.*)

PHILIP. (*Soothing a silly mother.*) No, mother, don't! But I shall expect you, of course, at the ceremony. (MRS. PHILLIMORE *exits* R. PHILIP *comes down* C. PHILIP *takes the tone and assumes the attitude of the injured husband.*) It is proper for me to tell you that I followed you to Belmont. I am aware—I know with whom—in fact, *I know all!* (*Pauses. He indicates the whole censorious universe.*) And now let me assure you—I am the last man in the world to be jilted on the very eve of— of—everything with you. I won't be jilted. (CYNTHIA *is silent.*) You understand? I propose to marry you. I won't be made ridiculous.

CYNTHIA. (*Glancing at* PHILIP, R.) Philip, I didn't mean to make you—

PHILIP. Why, then, did you run off to Belmont Park with that fellow?

CYNTHIA. Philip, I—eh—

PHILIP. (*Sits right of table,* R.) What motive? What reason? On our wedding day? Why did you do it?

CYNTHIA. I'll tell you the truth. I was bored.

PHILIP. Bored? In my company? (PHILIP, *in a gesture, gives up.*)

CYNTHIA. I was bored, and then—and besides, Sir Wilfrid asked me to go.

PHILIP. Exactly, and that was why you went. Cynthia, when you promised to marry me, you told me you had forever done with love. You agreed that marriage was the rational coming together of two people.

CYNTHIA. I know, I know!

PHILIP. Do you believe that now?

CYNTHIA. I don't know what I believe. My brain is in a whirl! But, Philip, I am beginning to be—I'm afraid—yes, I am afraid that one can't just select a great and good man (*She indicates him.*) and say: I will be happy with him.

PHILIP. (*With dignity.*) I don't see why not. You must assuredly do one or the other: You must either let your heart choose or your head select.

CYNTHIA. (*Gravely.*) No, there's a third scheme; Sir Wilfrid explained the theory to me. A woman should marry whenever she has a whim for the man, and then leave the rest to the man. Do you see?

PHILIP. (*Furious.*) Do I see? Have I ever seen anything else? Marry for whim! That's the New York idea of marriage.

CYNTHIA. (*Giving a cynical opinion.*) New York ought to know.

PHILIP. Marry for whim and leave the rest to the divorce court! Marry for whim and leave the rest to the man. That was the former Mrs. Phillimore's idea. Only she spelled "whim" differently; she omitted the "w." (*He rises in his anger.*) And now you—*you* take up with this preposterous— (CYNTHIA *moves uneasily.*) But, nonsense! It's impossible! A woman of your mental calibre—No. Some obscure, primitive, female *feeling* is at work corrupting your better judgment! What is it you *feel?*

CYNTHIA. Philip, you never felt like a fool, did you?

PHILIP. No, never.

CYNTHIA. (*Politely.*) I thought not.

PHILIP. No, but whatever your feelings, I conclude you are ready to marry me.

CYNTHIA. (*Uneasy.*) Of course, I came back. I am here, am I not?

PHILIP. You are ready to marry me?

CYNTHIA. (*Twisting in the coils.*) But you haven't had your dinner.

PHILIP. Do I understand you refuse?

CYNTHIA. Couldn't we defer—?

PHILIP. You refuse?

CYNTHIA. (*A slight pause; trapped and seeing no way out.*) No, I said I'd marry you. I'm a woman of my word. I will.

PHILIP. (*Triumphant.*) Ah! Very good, then. Run to your room. (CYNTHIA *turns to* PHILIP.) Throw something over you. In a half hour I'll expect you here! And Cynthia, my dear, remember! I cannot cuculate like a wood pigeon, but—I esteem you!

CYNTHIA. (*Hopelessly.*) I think I'll go, Philip.

PHILIP. I may not be fitted to play the love-bird, but—

CYNTHIA. (*As before.*) I think I'll go, Philip.

PHILIP. I'll expect you,—in half an hour.

CYNTHIA. (*With leaden despair.*) Yes.

PHILIP. And, Cynthia, don't think any more about that fellow, Cates-Darby.

CYNTHIA. (*Amazed and disgusted by his misapprehension.*) No. (*Exit* CYNTHIA, R. THOMAS *enters from* L.)

PHILIP. (*Goes to* R. *table.*) And if I had that fellow, Cates-Darby, in the dock—!

THOMAS. Sir Wilfrid Cates-Darby.

PHILIP. Sir what—what—wh-who? (*Enter* SIR WILFRID, L. *in evening dress. Tableau.* PHILIP *looks* SIR WILFRID *in the face and speaks to* THOMAS.) Tell Sir Wilfrid Cates-Darby I am not at home to him. (THOMAS *embarrassed.*)

SIR WILFRID. (*Undaunted.*) My dear Lord Eldon—

PHILIP. (R., *to* THOMAS, *as before.*) Show the gentleman the door. (*Pause.* SIR WILFRID *glances at door* R., *and gesture.*)

SIR WILFRID. (*Goes to the door, examines it and returns to* PHILIP.) Eh,—I admire the door, my boy! Fine, old carved mahogany panel; but don't ask me to leave by it, for Mrs. Karslake made me promise I'd come, and that's why I'm here. (THOMAS *exits*, L.)

PHILIP. Sir, you are—impudent—!

SIR WILFRID. (*Interrupting.*) Ah, you put it all in a nutshell, don't you?

PHILIP. To show your face here, after practically eloping with my wife!

SIR WILFRID. (*Pretending ignorance.*) When were you married?

PHILIP. We are as good as married.

SIR WILFRID. Oh, pooh, pooh! You can't tell me that grace before soup is as good as a dinner! (*Takes cigar-case out; business of a dry smoke.*)

PHILIP. Sir—I—demand—

SIR WILFRID. (*Calmly carrying the situation.*) Mrs. Karslake is *not* married. *That's* why I'm here. I am here for the same purpose *you* are; to ask Mrs. Karslake to be my wife.

PHILIP. Are you in your senses?

SIR WILFRID. (*Touching up his American cousin in his pet vanity.*) Come, come, Judge—you Americans have no sense of humor. (*He takes a small jewel-case from his pocket.*) There's my regards for the lady—and (*Reasonably.*) if I must go, I will. Of course, I would like to see her, but—if it isn't your American custom— (*Enter* THOMAS.)

THOMAS. Mr. Karslake.

SIR WILFRID. Oh, well, I say; if he can come, I can! (*Enter* JOHN KARSLAKE *in evening dress, carrying a large and very smart bride's bouquet which he hands to*

PHILIP. PHILIP *takes it because he isn't up to dropping it, but gets it out of his hands as soon as he can.* PHILIP *is transfixed;* JOHN *comes down* C. *Deep down he is feeling wounded and unhappy. But, as he knows his coming to the ceremony on whatever pretext is a social outrage, he carries it off by assuming an air of its being the most natural thing in the world. He controls the expression of his deeper emotion, but the pressure of this keeps his face grave, and he speaks with force.*)

JOHN. My compliments to the bride, Judge.

PHILIP. (*Angry.*) And you, too, have the effrontery?

SIR WILFRID. There you are!

JOHN. (*Pretending ease.*) Oh, call it friendship— (THOMAS *exits* L.)

PHILIP. (*Puts bouquet on table. Ironically.*) I suppose Mrs. Karslake—

JOHN. She wagered me I wouldn't give her away, and of course— (*Throughout this scene* JOHN *hides the emotions he will not show behind a daring irony. He has* PHILIP *on his left, walking about in a fury:* SIR WILFRID *sits on the edge of the table, gay and undisturbed.*)

PHILIP. (*A step toward* JOHN.) You will oblige me— both of you—by immediately leaving—

JOHN. (*Smiles and goes to* PHILIP.) Oh, come, come, Judge—suppose I *am* here? Who has a better right to attend his wife's obsequies! Certainly, I come as a mourner—for *you!*

SIR WILFRID. I say, is it the custom?

JOHN. No, no—of course it's not the custom, no. But we'll make it the custom. After all,—what's a divorced wife among friends?

PHILIP. Sir, your humor is strained!

JOHN. Humor,—Judge?

PHILIP. It is, sir, and I'll not be bantered! Your both being here is—it is—gentlemen, there is a decorum which the stars in their courses do not violate.

JOHN. Now, Judge, never you mind what the stars do in their divorces! Get down to earth of the present day. Rufus Choate and Daniel Webster are dead. You must be modern. You must let peroration and poetry alone! Come along now. Why shouldn't I give the lady away?

SIR WILFRID. Hear! Hear! Oh, I beg your pardon!

JOHN. And why shouldn't we both be here? American marriage is a new thing. We've got to strike the pace, and the only trouble is, Judge, that the judiciary have so messed the thing up that a man can't be sure he *is* married until he's divorced. It's a sort of merry-go-round, to be sure! But let it go at that! Here we all are, and we're ready to marry my wife to you, and start her on her way to him!

PHILIP. (*Brought to a standstill.*) Good Lord! Sir, you cannot trifle with monogamy!

JOHN. Now, now, Judge, monogamy is just as extinct as knee-breeches. The new woman has a new idea, and the new idea is—well, it's just the opposite of the old Mormon one. Their idea is one man, ten wives and a hundred children. Our idea is one woman, a hundred husbands and one child.

PHILIP. Sir, this is polyandry.

JOHN. Polyandry? A hundred to one it's polyandry; and that's it, Judge! Uncle Sam has established consecutive polyandry,—but there's got to be an interval between husbands! The fact is, Judge, the modern American marriage is like a wire fence. The woman's the wire—the posts are the husbands. (*He indicates himself, and then* SIR WILFRID *and* PHILIP.) One—two—three! And if you cast your eye over the future you can count them, post after post, up hill, down dale, all the way to Dakota!

PHILIP. All very amusing, sir, but the fact remains—

JOHN. (*Goes to* PHILIP, R. PHILIP *moves to* R.) Now, now, Judge, I like you. But you're asleep; you're living in the dark ages. You want to call up Central. "Hello, Central! Give me the present time, 1906, New York!"

SIR WILFRID. Of course you do, and—there you are!

PHILIP. There I am not, sir! And— (*To* JOHN.) as for Mr. Karslake's ill-timed jocosity,—sir, in the future—

SIR WILFRID. Oh, hang the future!

PHILIP. I begin to hope, Sir Wilfrid, that in the future I shall have the pleasure of hanging you! (*To* JOHN.) And as to you, sir, your insensate idea of giving away your own—your former—my—your—oh! Good Lord! This is a nightmare! (*He turns to go in despair. Enter* MATTHEW, *who, seeing* PHILIP, *speaks as he comes in from door* R.)

MATTHEW. (*To* PHILIP.) My dear brother, Aunt Sarah Heneage refuses to give Mrs. Karslake away, unless you yourself, —eh—

PHILIP. (*As he exits.*) No more! I'll attend to the matter! (*Exit*, R. *The choir boys are heard practicing in the next room.*)

MATTHEW. (*Mopping his brow.*) How do you both do? My aunt has made me very warm. (*He rings the bell.*) You hear our choir practicing—sweet angel boys! Hm! Hm! Some of the family will not be present. I am very fond of you, Mr. Karslake, and I think it admirably Christian of you to have waived your—eh—your—eh— that is, now that I look at it more narrowly, let me say, that in the excitement of pleasurable anticipation, I forgot, Karslake, that your presence might occasion remark— (*Enter* THOMAS.) Thomas! I left, in the hall, a small handbag or satchel containing my surplice.

THOMAS. Yes, sir. Ahem!

MATTHEW. You must really find the handbag at once. (THOMAS *turns to go, when he stops startled.*)

THOMAS. Yes, sir. (*Announcing in consternation.*)

Mrs. Vida Phillimore. (*Enter* VIDA PHILLIMORE, *in full evening dress. She steps gently to* MATTHEW.)

MATTHEW. (*Always piously serene.*) Ah, my dear child! Now this is just as it should be! That is, eh— (*He comes* C. *with her; she pointedly looks away from* SIR WILFRID.) That is, when I come to think of it—your presence might be deemed inauspicious.

VIDA. But, my dear Matthew,—I had to come. (*Aside to him.*) I have a reason for being here. (THOMAS *enters from* R.)

MATTHEW. But, my dear child— (*Gesture.*)

THOMAS. (*With sympathetic intention.*) Sir, Mr. Phillimore wishes to have your assistance, sir—with Miss Heneage *immediately!*

MATTHEW. Ah! (*To* VIDA.) One moment! I'll return. (*To* THOMAS.) Have you found the bag with my surplice? (*He goes out* L., *with* THOMAS, *speaking.* SIR WILFRID *comes to* VIDA. JOHN *crosses and comes down* R. *and watches door up* L.)

SIR WILFRID. (*To* VIDA.) You're just the person I most want to see!

VIDA. (*With affected iciness.*) Oh, no, Sir Wilfrid, Cynthia isn't here yet! (*Crosses* R., *to table.* JOHN *comes down right of table* R. *To him, with obvious sweetness.*) Jack, dear, I never was so ravished to see any one.

SIR WILFRID. (*Taken aback.*) By Jove!

VIDA. (*Very sweet.*) I knew I should find you here?

JOHN. (*Annoyed but civil.*) Now don't do that!

VIDA. (*As before.*) Jack! (*They sit.*)

JOHN. (*Civil but plain spoken.*) Don't do it!

VIDA. (*In a voice dripping with honey.*) Do what, Jack?

JOHN. Touch me with your voice! I have troubles enough of my own. (*He sits not far from her; the table between them.*)

VIDA. And I know *who* your troubles are! Cynthia! (*From this moment* VIDA *gives up* JOHN *as an object of the chase and lets him into her other game.*)

JOHN. I hate her. I don't know why I came.

VIDA. You came, dear, because you couldn't stay away—you're in love with her.

JOHN. All right, Vida, what I feel may be *love*—but all I can say is, if I could get even with Cynthia Karslake—

VIDA. You can, dear—it's as easy as powdering one's face; all you have to do is to be too nice to me!

JOHN. (*Looks inquiringly at* VIDA.) Eh!

VIDA. Don't you realize she's jealous of you? Why did she come to my house this morning? She's jealous—and all you have to do—

JOHN. If I can make her wince, I'll make love to you till the Heavenly cows come home!

VIDA. Well, you see, my dear, if you make love to me it will (*She delicately indicates* SIR WILFRID.) cut both ways at once!

JOHN. Eh,—what! Not Cates-Darby? (*Starts.*) Is that Cynthia?

VIDA. Now don't get rattled and forget to make love to me.

JOHN. I've got the jumps. (*Trying to accept her instructions.*) Vida, I adore you.

VIDA. Oh, you must be more convincing; that won't do at all.

JOHN. (*Listens.*) Is that she now? (*Enter* MATTHEW, *who goes to the inner room.*)

VIDA. It's Matthew. And, Jack, dear, you'd best get the hang of it before Cynthia comes. You might tell me all about your divorce. That's a sympathetic subject. Were you able to undermine it?

JOHN. No. I've got a wire from my lawyer this morning. The divorce holds. She's a free woman. She can marry whom she likes. (*The organ is heard, very softly played.*) Is that Cynthia? (*Rises quickly.*)

VIDA. It's the organ!

JOHN. (*Overwhelmingly excited.*) By George! I should never have come! I think I'll go. (*He crosses to go to the door.*)

VIDA. (*She rises and follows him remonstratingly.*) When I need you?

JOHN. I can't stand it.

VIDA. Oh, but, Jack—

JOHN. Good-night!

VIDA. I feel quite ill. (*Seeing that she must play her last card to keep him, pretends to faintness; sways and falls into his arms.*) Oh!

JOHN. (*In a rage, but beaten.*) I believe you're putting up a fake. (*The organ swells as* CYNTHIA *enters sweepingly, dressed in full evening dress for the wedding ceremony. Tableau.* JOHN, *not knowing what to do, holds* VIDA *up as a horrid necessity.*)

CYNTHIA. (*Speaking as she comes on, to* MATTHEW.) Here I am. Ridiculous to make it a conventional thing, you know. Come in on the swell of the music, and all that, just as if I'd never been married before. Where's Philip? (*She looks for* PHILIP *and sees* JOHN *with* VIDA *in his arms. She stops short.*)

JOHN. (*Uneasy and embarrassed.*) A glass of water! I beg your pardon, Mrs. Karslake— (*The organ plays on.*)

CYNTHIA. (*Ironical and calm.*) Vida!

JOHN. She has fainted.

CYNTHIA. (*As before.*) Fainted? (*Without pause.*) Dear, dear, dear, terrible! So she has. (SIR WILFRID *takes flowers from a vase and prepares to sprinkle* VIDA'S *forehead with the water it contains.*) No, no, not her forehead, Sir Wilfrid, her frock! Sprinkle her best Paquin! If it's a real faint, she will not come to!

VIDA. (*As her Paris importation is about to suffer comes to her senses.*) I almost fainted.

CYNTHIA. Almost!

VIDA. (*Using the stock phrase as a matter of course, and reviving rapidly.*) Where am I? (JOHN *glances at* CYNTHIA *sharply.*) Oh, the bride! I beg every one's pardon. Cynthia, at a crisis like this, I simply couldn't stay away from Philip!

CYNTHIA. Stay away from Philip? (JOHN *and* CYNTHIA *exchange glances.*)

VIDA. Your arm, Jack; and lead me where there is air. (JOHN *and* VIDA *go into the further room;* JOHN *stands left of her. The organ stops.* SIR WILFRID *comes down. He and* CYNTHIA *are practically alone on the stage.* JOHN *and* VIDA *are barely within sight. You first see him take her fan and give her air; then he picks up a book and reads from it to her.*)

SIR WILFRID. I've come back.

CYNTHIA. (*To* SIR WILFRID.) Asks for air and goes to the greenhouse. (CYNTHIA *crosses* L. SIR WILFRID *offers her a seat.*) I know why you are here. It's that intoxicating little whim you suppose me to have for you. My regrets! But the whim's gone flat! Yes, yes, my gasoline days are over. I'm going to be garaged for good. However, I'm glad you're here; you take the edge off—

SIR WILFRID. Mr. Phillimore?

CYNTHIA. (*Sharply.*) No, Karslake. I'm just waiting to say the words (*Enter* THOMAS.) "love, honor and obey" to Phillimore— (*Looks up back.*) and *at* Karslake! (CYNTHIA *sees* THOMAS.) What is it? Mr. Phillimore?

THOMAS. Mr. Phillimore will be down in a few minutes, ma'am. He's very sorry, ma'am, (*Lowers his voice and comes nearer* CYNTHIA, *mindful of the respectabilities.*) but there's a button off his waistcoat.

CYNTHIA. (*Rises, crossing* L.) Button off his waistcoat! (*Exit* THOMAS, L.)

SIR WILFRID. (*Delightedly.*) Ah! So much the better for me. (CYNTHIA *looks up back.*) Now, then, never mind those two! (CYNTHIA *moves restlessly.*) Sit down.

CYNTHIA. I can't.

SIR WILFRID. You're as nervous as—

CYNTHIA. Nervous! Of course I'm nervous! So would you be nervous if you'd had had a runaway and smash up, and you were going to try it again. (*Looks up back.* SIR WILFRID *uneasy.*) And if some one doesn't do away with those calla lilies—the odor makes me faint! (SIR WILFRID *moves.*) No, it's not the lilies! It's the orange blossoms!

SIR WILFRID. Orange blossoms.

CYNTHIA. The flowers that grow on the tree that hangs over the abyss! (SIR WILFRID *gets the vase of orange blossoms.*) They smell of six o'clock in the evening. When Philip's fallen asleep, and little boys are crying the winners outside, and I'm crying inside, and dying inside and outside and everywhere. (SIR WILFRID *comes down.*)

SIR WILFRID. Sorry to disappoint you. They're artificial. (CYNTHIA *shrugs her shoulders.*) That's it! They're emblematic of artificial domesticity! And I'm here to help you balk it. (*He sits;* CYNTHIA *half rises and looks toward* JOHN *and* VIDA.) Keep still now, I've a lot to say to you. Stop looking—

CYNTHIA. Do you think I can listen to you make love to me when the man who—who—whom I most despise in all the world, is reading poetry to the woman who—who got me into the fix I'm in!

SIR WILFRID. (*Leaning over the chair in which she*

sits.) What do you want to look at 'em for? (CYNTHIA *moves.*) Let 'em be and listen to me! Sit down; for damme, I'm determined. (CYNTHIA *sits right of table* R.)

CYNTHIA. (*Half to herself.*) I won't look at them! I won't think of them. Beasts! (SIR WILFRID *interposes between her and her view of* JOHN. *Enter* THOMAS, *who comes down* R.)

SIR WILFRID. Now, then— (*He sits.*)

CYNTHIA. Those two *here!* It's just as if Adam and Eve should invite the snake to their golden wedding. (*She sees* THOMAS.) What is it, what's the matter?

THOMAS. Mr. Phillimore's excuses, ma'am. In a very short time— (THOMAS *exits,* R. *door.*)

SIR WILFRID. I'm on to you! You hoped for more buttons!

CYNTHIA. I'm dying of the heat; fan me. (SIR WILFRID *fans* CYNTHIA.)

SIR WILFRID. Heat! No! You're dying because you're ignorin' nature. Certainly you are! You're marryin' Phillimore! (CYNTHIA, *business; feels faint.*) Can't ignore nature, Mrs. Karslake. Yes, you are; you're forcin' your feelin's. (CYNTHIA *glances at him.*) And what you want to do is to let yourself go a bit—up anchor and sit tight! I'm no seaman, but that's the idea! (CYNTHIA *moves and shakes her head.*) So just throw the reins on nature's neck, jump this fellow Phillimore and marry me! (*He leans over to* CYNTHIA.)

CYNTHIA. (*Naturally and irritably.*) You propose to me here, at a moment like this? When I'm on the last lap—just in sight of the goal—the gallows—the halter —the altar, I don't know what its name is! No, I won't have you! (*Looking toward* KARSLAKE *and* VIDA.) And I won't have you stand near me! I won't have you talking to me in a low tone! (*As before.*) Stand over there— stand where you are.

SIR WILFRID. I say—

CYNTHIA. I can hear you—I'm listening!

SIR WILFRID. Well, don't look so hurried and worried. You've got buttons and buttons of time. And now my offer. You haven't yet said you would—

CYNTHIA. Marry you? I don't even know you!

SIR WILFRID. (*Feeling sure of being accepted.*) Oh, —tell you all about myself. I'm no duke in a pickle o' debts, d'ye see? I can marry where I like. Some o' my countrymen are rotters, ye know. They'd marry a monkey, if poppa-up-the-tree had a corner in cocoanuts! And they do marry some queer ones, y' know. (CYNTHIA *looks up, exclaims and turns.* SIR WILFRID *turns.*)

CYNTHIA. Do they?

SIR WILFRID. Oh, rather. That's what's giving your heiresses such a bad name lately. If a fellah's in debt he can't pick and choose, and then he swears that American gals are awfully fine lookers, but they're no good when it comes to continuin' the race! Fair dolls in the drawin'-room, but no good in the nursery.

CYNTHIA. (*Thinking of* JOHN *and* VIDA *and nothing else.*) I can see Vida in the nursery.

SIR WILFRID. You understand when you want a brood mare, you don't choose a Kentucky mule.

CYNTHIA. I think I see one.

SIR WILFRID. Well, that's what they're saying over there. They say your gals run to talk, (*He plainly remembers* VIDA's *volubility.*) and I have seen gals here that would chat life into a wooden Indian! That's what you Americans call being clever.—All brains and no stuffin'! In fact, some of your American gals are the nicest boys I ever met.

CYNTHIA. So that's what you think?

SIR WILFRID. Not a bit what *I* think—what my countrymen think!

CYNTHIA. Why are you telling me?

SIR WILFRID. Oh, just explaining my character. I'm the sort that can pick and choose—and what I want is heart.

CYNTHIA. (*Always* VIDA *and* JOHN *in mind.*) No more heart than a dragon-fly! (*The organ begins to play softly.*)

SIR WILFRID. That's it, dragon-fly. Cold as stone and never stops buzzing about and showin' off her colors. It's that American dragon-fly girl that I'm afraid of, because d'ye see, I don't know what an American expects when he marries; yes, but you're not listening!

CYNTHIA. I am listening. I am!

SIR WILFRID. (*Speaks directly to her.*) An Englishman, ye see, when he marries expects three things; love, obedience and five children.

CYNTHIA. Three things! I make it seven!

SIR WILFRID. Yes, my dear, but the point is, will you be mistress of Traynham?

CYNTHIA. (*Who has only half listened to him.*) No, Sir Wilfrid, thank you, I won't. (*She turns to see* JOHN *crossing the drawing-room at back, with* VIDA, *apparently absorbed in what she says.*) It's outrageous!

SIR WILFRID. Eh? Why you're cryin'?

CYNTHIA. (*Almost sobbing.*) I am not.

SIR WILFRID. You're not crying because you're in love with me?

CYNTHIA. I'm not crying—or if I am, I'm crying because I love my country. It's a disgrace to America— cast-off husbands and wives getting together in a parlor and playing tag under a palm-tree. (JOHN *with intention and determined to stab* CYNTHIA, *kisses* VIDA'S *hand.*)

SIR WILFRID. Eh! Oh! I'm damned! (*To* CYNTHIA.) What do you think that means?

CYNTHIA. I don't doubt it means a wedding here, at once—after mine! (VIDA *and* JOHN *come down.*)

VIDA. (*Affecting an impossible intimacy to wound* CYNTHIA *and tantalize* SIR WILFRID.) Hush, Jack—I'd much rather no one should know anything about it until it's all over!

CYNTHIA. (*Starts and looks at* SIR WILFRID.) What did I tell you?

VIDA. (*To* CYNTHIA.) Oh, my dear, he's asked me to champagne and lobster at *your* house—his house! Matthew is coming! (CYNTHIA *starts, but controls herself.*) And you're to come, Sir Wilfrid. (VIDA *speaks, intending to convey the idea of a sudden marriage ceremony.*) Of course, my dear, I would like to wait for your wedding, but something rather—rather important to me is to take place, and I know you'll excuse me. (*Organ stops.*)

SIR WILFRID. (*Piqued at being forgotten.*) All very neat, but you haven't given me a chance, even.

VIDA. Chance? You're not serious?

SIR WILFRID. I am!

VIDA. (*Striking while the iron is hot.*) I'll give you a minute to offer yourself.

SIR WILFRID. Eh?

VIDA. Sixty seconds from now.

SIR WILFRID. (*Uncertain.*) There's such a thing as bein' silly.

VIDA. (*Calm and determined.*) Fifty seconds left.

SIR WILFRID. I take you—count fair. (*He hands her his watch and goes to where* CYNTHIA *stands.*) I say, Mrs. Karslake—

CYNTHIA. (*Overwhelmed with grief and emotion.*) They're engaged; they're going to be married to-night, over champagne and lobster at my house!

SIR WILFRID. Will you consider your—

CYNTHIA. (*Hastily, to get rid of him.*) No, no, no, no! Thank you, Sir Wilfrid, I will not.

SIR WILFRID. (*Calm, and not to be laid low.*) Thanks awfully. (*Crosses to* VIDA. CYNTHIA *goes up.*) Mrs. Phillimore—

VIDA. (*She gives him back his watch.*) Too late! (*To* KARSLAKE.) Jack, dear, we must be off.

SIR WILFRID. (*Standing* C. *and making a general appeal for information.*) I say, is it the custom for American girls—that sixty seconds or too late? Look here! Not a bit too late. I'll take you around to Jack Karslake's, and I'm going to ask you the same old question again, you know. (*To* VIDA.) By Jove, you know in your country it's the pace that kills. (*Exeunt* SIR WILFRID *and* VIDA, L. *door.*)

JOHN. (*Gravely to* CYNTHIA, *who comes down.*) Good-night, Mrs. Karslake, I'm going; I'm sorry I came.

CYNTHIA. Sorry? Why are you sorry? (JOHN *looks at her; she winces a little.*) You've got what you wanted. (*Pause.*) I wouldn't mind your marrying Vida—

JOHN. (*Gravely.*) Oh, wouldn't you?

CYNTHIA. But I don't think you showed good taste in engaging yourselves *here*.

JOHN. Of course, I should have preferred a garden of roses and plenty of twilight.

CYNTHIA. (*Rushing into speech.*) I'll tell you what you *have* done—you've thrown yourself away! A woman like that! No head, no heart! All languor and loose—loose frocks—she's the typical, worst thing America can do! She's the regular American marriage worm!

JOHN. I have known others—

CYNTHIA. (*Quickly.*) Not me. I'm not a patch on that woman. Do you know anything about her life? Do you know the things she did to Philip? Kept him up every night of his life—forty days out of every thirty—and then, without his knowing it, put brandy in his coffee to make him lively at breakfast.

JOHN. (*Banteringly.*) I begin to think she is just the woman—

CYNTHIA. (*Unable to quiet her jealously.*) She is *not* the woman for *you!* A man with your bad temper—your airs of authority—your assumption of—of—everything. What you need is a good, old-fashioned, bread poultice woman! (CYNTHIA, *full stop; faces* JOHN.)

JOHN. (*Sharply.*) Can't say I've had any experience of the good old-fashioned bread poultice.

CYNTHIA. I don't care what you say! If you marry Vida Phillimore—you shan't do it. (*Tears of rage choking her.*) No, I liked your father and for *his* sake, I'll see that his son doesn't make a donkey of himself a second time.

JOHN. (*Too angry to be amused.*) Oh, I thought I was divorced. I begin to feel as if I had you on my hands still.

CYNTHIA. You have! You shall have! If you attempt to marry her, I'll follow you—and I'll find her—I'll tell Vida— (*He turns to her.*) I will. I'll tell Vida just what sort of a dance you led me.

JOHN. (*Quickly on her last word but speaking gravely.*) Indeed! Will you? And *why* do you care what happens to me?

CYNTHIA. (*Startled by his tone.*) I—I—ah—

JOHN. (*Insistently and with a faint hope.*) *Why* do you *care?*

CYNTHIA. I don't. Not in your sense—

JOHN. How dare you then pretend—

CYNTHIA. I don't pretend.

JOHN. (*Interrupting her; proud, serious and strong.*) How dare you look me in the face with the eyes that I once kissed, and pretend the least regard for me? (CYNTHIA *recoils and looks away. Her own feelings are revealed to her clearly for the first time.*) I begin to understand our American women now. Fire-flies—and the fire they gleam with is so cold that a midge couldn't warm his heart at it, let alone a man. You're not of the same race as a man! You married me for nothing, divorced me for nothing, because you *are* nothing!

CYNTHIA. (*Wounded to the heart.*) Jack! What are you saying?

JOHN. (*With unrestrained emotion.*) What,—you feigning an interest in me, feigning a lie—and in five minutes— (*Gesture indicating altar.*) Oh, you've taught me the trick of your sex—you're the woman who's not a woman!

CYNTHIA. (*Weakly.*) You're saying terrible things to me.

JOHN. (*Low and with intensity.*) You haven't been divorced from me long enough to forget—what you should be ashamed to remember.

CYNTHIA. (*Unable to face him and pretending not to understand him.*) I don't know what you mean?

JOHN. (*More forcibly and with manly emotion.*) You're not able to forget me? You know you're not able to forget me; ask yourself if you are able to forget me, and when your heart, such as it is, answers "no," then— (*The organ is plainly heard.*) Well, then, prance gaily up to the altar and marry that, if you can! (*He exits quickly,* L. CYNTHIA *crosses to armchair and sinks into it. She trembles as if she were overdone. Voices are heard speaking in the next room. Enter* MATTHEW *and* MISS HENEAGE, R. *Enter* PHILIP, R. CYNTHIA *is so sunk in the chair they do not see her.* MISS HENEAGE *goes up to sofa back and waits. They all are* **dressed** *for an*

ACT III THE NEW YORK IDEA 103

evening reception and PHILIP *in the traditional bridegroom's rig—large buttonhole, etc.*)

MATTHEW. (*As he enters.*) I am sure you will do your part, Sarah—in a spirit of Christian decorum. (*To* PHILIP.) It was impossible to find my surplice, Philip, but the more informal the better.

PHILIP. (*With pompous responsibility.*) Where's Cynthia? (MATTHEW *gives glance around room.*)

MATTHEW. Ah, here's the choir! (*Goes up stage. Choir boys come in very orderly; divide and take their places, an even number on each side of the altar of flowers.* MATTHEW *vaguely superintends.* PHILIP *gets in the way of the bell. Moves out of the way. Enter* THOMAS.) Thomas, I directed you—One moment if you please. (*Indicates table and chairs.* THOMAS *hastens to move chairs and table* L. *against wall.* PHILIP *comes down.*)

PHILIP. (*Looking for her.*) Where's Cynthia? (CYNTHIA *rises.* PHILIP *sees her when she moves and crosses toward her, but stops. Organ stops.*)

CYNTHIA. (*Faintly.*) Here I am. (MATTHEW *comes down. Organ plays softly.*)

MATTHEW. (*Coming to* CYNTHIA.) Ah, my very dear Cynthia, I knew there was something. Let me tell you the words of the hymn I have chosen:

"Enduring love; sweet end of strife!
Oh, bless this happy man and wife!"

I'm afraid you feel—eh—eh!

CYNTHIA. (*Desperately calm.*) I feel awfully queer—I think I need a scotch. (*Organ stops.* PHILIP *remains uneasily up* L. MRS. PHILLIMORE *and* GRACE *enter back slowly, as cheerfully as if they were going to hear the funeral service read. They remain up* L.)

MATTHEW. Really, my dear, in the pomp and vanity —I mean—ceremony of this—this unique occasion, there should be sufficient exhilaration.

CYNTHIA. (*As before.*) But there isn't! (*She sits.*)
MATTHEW. I don't think my Bishop would approve of —eh—anything *before!*
CYNTHIA. (*Too agitated to know how much she is moved.*) I feel very queer.
MATTHEW. (*Piously sure that everything is for the best.*) My dear child—
CYNTHIA. However, I suppose there's nothing for it—now—but—to—to—
MATTHEW. Courage!
CYNTHIA. (*Desperate and with sudden explosion.*) Oh, don't speak to me. I feel as if I'd been eating gunpowder, and the very first word of the wedding service would set it off!
MATTHEW. My dear, your indisposition is the voice of nature. (CYNTHIA *speaks more rapidly and with growing excitement.* MATTHEW *goes up to* C. *and near the choir boys.*)
CYNTHIA. Ah,—that's it—nature! (MATTHEW *shakes his head.*) I've a great mind to throw the reins on nature's neck.
PHILIP. Matthew! (*He moves to take his stand for the ceremony.*)
MATTHEW. (*Looks at* PHILIP. *To* CYNTHIA.) Philip is ready. (PHILIP *comes down* C. *The organ plays the wedding march.*)
CYNTHIA. (*To herself, as if at bay.*) Ready? Ready? Ready?
MATTHEW. Cynthia, you will take Miss Heneage's arm. (MISS HENEAGE *comes down near table.*) Sarah! (MATTHEW *indicates to* MISS HENEAGE *where* CYNTHIA *is.* MISS HENEAGE *advances a step or two.* MATTHEW *goes up* C., *and speaks in a low voice to choir.*) Now please don't forget, my boys. When I raise my hands so, you begin, "Enduring love, sweet end of strife," etc.

(CYNTHIA *has risen. On the table is her long lace cloak. She stands by this table.* MATTHEW *assumes sacerdotal importance and takes his position inside the altar of flowers.*) Ahem! Philip! (*He indicates to* PHILIP *to take his position.*) Sarah! (CYNTHIA *breathes fast, and supports herself on table.* MISS HENEAGE *goes down* L. *and stands for a moment looking at* CYNTHIA.) The ceremony will now begin. (*The organ plays Mendelssohn's wedding march.* CYNTHIA *turns and faces* MISS HENEAGE. MISS HENEAGE *comes* C. *slowly, and extends her hand in her readiness to lead the bride to the altar.*)

MISS HENEAGE. Mrs. Karslake!

PHILIP. Ahem! (MATTHEW *steps forward two or three steps.* CYNTHIA *stands turned to stone.*)

MATTHEW. My dear Cynthia. I request you—to take your place. (CYNTHIA *moves one or two steps across as if to go up to the altar. She takes* MISS HENEAGE'S *hand and slowly they walk toward* MATTHEW.) Your husband to be—is ready, the ring is in my pocket. I have only to ask you the—eh—necessary questions,—and—eh—all will be blissfully over in a moment. (*The organ is louder.*)

CYNTHIA. (*At this moment, just as she reaches* PHILIP, *she stops, faces round, looks him,* MATTHEW *and the rest in the face and cries out in despair.*) Thomas! Call a hansom! (THOMAS *exits and leaves door open.* MISS HENEAGE *crosses* L. MRS. PHILLIMORE *rises.* CYNTHIA *grasps her cloak on table* R. PHILIP *turns and* CYNTHIA *comes right of* C. *and stops.*) I can't, Philip— I can't. (*Whistle of hansom is heard off; the organ stops.*) It is simply a case of throwing the reins on nature's neck—up anchor—and sit tight! (MATTHEW *crosses to* CYNTHIA.) Matthew, don't come near me! Yes, yes, I distrust you. It's your business, and you'd marry me if you could.

PHILIP. (*Watching her in dismay as she throws on her cloak.*) Where are you going?

CYNTHIA. I'm going to Jack.

PHILIP. What for?

CYNTHIA. To stop his marrying Vida. I'm blowing a hurricane inside, a horrible, happy hurricane! I know myself—I know what's the matter with me. If I married you and Miss Heneage—what's the use of talking about it—he mustn't marry that woman. He shan't. (CYNTHIA *has now all her wraps on; goes up rapidly. To* PHILIP.) Sorry! So long! Good-night and see you later. (CYNTHIA *goes to door* R., *rapidly;* MATTHEW, *in absolute amazement, throws up his arms.* PHILIP *is rigid.* MRS. PHILLIMORE *sinks into a chair.* MISS HENEAGE *supercilious and unmoved.* GRACE *the same. The choir, at* MATTHEW'S *gesture, mistakes it for the concerted signal, and bursts lustily into the Epithalamis.*)

"Enduring love—sweet end of strife!
Oh, bless this happy man and wife!"

CURTAIN

ACT FOUR

SCENE: JOHN KARSLAKE'S *study and smoking-room. Bay window up* R. *Door* R. *to stairs and the front door of house. Door* L., *at back, leading to the dining-room. Fireplace down* L., *and mantel. 'Phone down* L. *Bookcase containing law books and sporting books. Full-length portrait of* CYNTHIA *on the wall,* R. *Nothing of this portrait is seen by audience except the gilt frame and a space of canvas. A large table with writing materials is littered over with law books, sporting books, papers, pipes, crops, a pair of spurs, etc. A wedding ring lies on it. There are three very low easy-chairs. The general appearance of the room is extremely gay and garish in color. It has the easy confusion of a man's room. A small table* R. *On this table is a woman's sewing-basket. The sewing-basket is open. A piece of rich fancy work lies on the table, as if a lady had just risen from sewing. On the corner are a lady's gloves. On a chair-back is a lady's hat. It is a half hour later than the close of Act III. Curtains are drawn over window. Lamp on table* L., *lighted. Electric lights about room also lighted. One chair down* R. *is conspicuously standing on its head.*

(*Curtain rises on* NOGAM, *who busies himself at table, back. Door at back is half open.*)

SIR WILFRID. (*Comes in door* L., *up.*) Eh—what did you say your name was?
NOGAM. Nogam, sir.

SIR WILFRID. Nogam? I've been here thirty minutes. Where are the cigars? (NOGAM *motions to a small table near the entrance door where the cigars are.*) Thank you. Nogam, Mr. Karslake was to have followed us here, immediately. (*He lights a cigar.*)

NOGAM. Mr. Karslake just now 'phoned from his club (SIR WILFRID *comes down* R.) and he's on his way home, sir.

SIR WILFRID. Nogam, why is that chair upside down?

NOGAM. Our orders, sir.

VIDA. (*Speaking as she comes on.*) Oh, Wilfrid! (SIR WILFRID *turns.* VIDA *comes slowly down.*) I can't be left longer alone with the lobster! He reminds me too much of Phillimore!

SIR WILFRID. Karslake's coming; stopped at his club on the way! (*To* NOGAM.) You haven't heard anything of Mrs. Karslake—?

NOGAM. (*Surprised.*) No, sir!

SIR WILFRID. (*In an aside to* VIDA, *as they move right to appear to be out of* NOGAM'S *hearing.*) Deucedly odd, ye know—for the Reverend Matthew declared she left Phillimore's house before *he* did,—and she told them she was coming here! (NOGAM *evidently takes this in.*)

VIDA. Oh, she'll turn up.

SIR WILFRID. Yes, but I don't see how the Reverend Phillimore had the time to get here and make us man and wife, don't y' know—

VIDA. Oh, Matthew had a fast horse and Cynthia a slow one—or she's a woman and changed her mind! Perhaps she's gone back and married Phillimore. And besides, dear, Matthew wasn't in the house four minutes and a half; only just long enough to hoop the hoop. (*She twirls her new wedding ring gently about her finger.*) Wasn't it lucky he had a ring in his pocket?

SIR WILFRID. Rather.

VIDA. And are you aware, dear, that Phillimore

bought and intended it for Cynthia? Do come (*She goes up to the door through which she entered.*) I'm desperately hungry! Whenever I'm married that's the effect it has! (VIDA *goes out.* SIR WILFRID *sees her through door, but stops to speak to* NOGAM.)

SIR WILFRID. We'll give Mr. Karslake ten minutes, Nogam. If he does not come then, you might serve supper. (*He follows* VIDA.)

NOGAM. (*To* SIR WILFRID.) Yes, sir. (*Door* R. *opens. Enter* FIDDLER.)

FIDDLER. (*Easy and business-like.*) Hello, Nogam, where's the guv'nor? That mare's off her oats, and I've got to see him.

NOGAM. He'll soon be here.

FIDDLER. Who was the parson I met leaving the house?

NOGAM. (*Whispers.*) Sir Wilfrid and Mrs. Phillimore have a date with the guv'nor in the dining-room, and the reverend gentleman— (*Gesture as of giving an ecclesiastical blessing.*)

FIDDLER. (*Amazed.*) He hasn't spliced them? (NOGAM *assents.*) He has? They're married? Never saw a parson could resist it!

NOGAM. Yes, but I've got another piece of news for you. Who do you think the Rev. Phillimore expected to find *here?*

FIDDLER. (*Proud of being in the know.*) Mrs. Karslake? I saw her headed this way in a hansom with a balky horse only a minute ago. If she hoped to be in at the finish— (FIDDLER *goes down* R. *and is about to set chair on its legs.*)

NOGAM. Mr. Fiddler, sir, please to let it alone.

FIDDLER. (*Puts chair down in surprise.*) Does it live on its blooming head?

NOGAM. Don't you remember? *She* threw it on its head when she left here, and he won't have it up. Ah, that's it—hat, sewing-basket and all,—the whole rig is to remain as it was when she handed him his knock-out. (*A bell rings outside.*)

FIDDLER. There's the guv'nor—I hear him!

NOGAM. I'll serve the supper. (*Takes letter from pocket and puts it on mantel.*) Mr. Fiddler, would you mind giving this to the guv'nor? It's from his lawyer—his lawyer couldn't find him and left it with me. He said it was very important. (*Goes up* L. *Bell rings again. Speaking off to* SIR WILFRID.) I'm coming, sir! (NOGAM *goes out back, and shuts door. Enter* JOHN KARSLAKE, R. *He looks downhearted, his hat is pushed over his eyes. His hands in his pockets. He enters slowly and heavily. Sees* FIDDLER, *who salutes, forgetting letter.* JOHN *comes* L. *and sits in armchair at study table.*)

JOHN. (*Speaking as he walks to his chair.*) Hello, Fiddler! (*Pause.* JOHN *throws himself into a chair, keeps his hat on. Throws down gloves; sighs.*)

FIDDLER. Came in to see you, sir, about Cynthia K.

JOHN. (*Drearily.*) Damn Cynthia K!—

FIDDLER. Couldn't have a word with you?

JOHN. (*Grumpy.*) No!

FIDDLER. Yes, sir.

JOHN. Fiddler.

FIDDLER. Yes, sir.

JOHN. Mrs. Karslake— (FIDDLER *nods.*) You used to say she was our mascot?

FIDDLER. Yes, sir.

JOHN. Well, she's just married herself to a—a sort of a man!

FIDDLER. Sorry to hear it, sir.

JOHN. Well, Fiddler, between you and me, we're a pair of idiots.

FIDDLER. Yes, sir!

JOHN. And now it's too late!

FIDDLER. Yes, sir—oh, beg your pardon, sir—your lawyer left a letter. (JOHN *takes letter; opens it and reads it, indifferently at first.*)

JOHN. (*As he opens letter.*) What's he got to say, more than what his wire said?—Eh— (*As he reads, he is dumbfounded.*) what?—Will explain.—Error in wording of telegram.—Call me up.— (*Turns to telephone quickly.*) The man can't mean that she's still—Hello! Hello! (JOHN *listens.*)

FIDDLER. Would like to have a word with you, sir—

JOHN. Hello, Central!

FIDDLER. That mare—

JOHN. (*Looks at letter; speaks into 'phone.*) 33246a 38! Did you get it?

FIDDLER. That mare, sir, she's got a touch of malaria—

JOHN. (*At the 'phone.*) Hello, Central—33246a—38! —Clayton Osgood—yes, yes, and say, Central—get a move on you!

FIDDLER. If you think well of it, sir, I'll give her a tonic—

JOHN. (*Still at the 'phone.*) Hello! Yes—yes—Jack Karslake. Is that you, Clayton? Yes—yes—well—

FIDDLER. Or if you like, sir, I'll give her—

JOHN. (*Turning on* FIDDLER.) Shut up! (*To 'phone.*) What was that? Not you—not you—a technical error? You mean to say that Mrs. Karslake is still—my— Hold the wire, Central—get off the wire! Get off the wire! Is that you, Clayton? Yes, yes—she and I are still —I got it! Good-bye! (*Hangs up receiver; falls back in chair. For a moment he is overcome. Takes up telephone book.*)

FIDDLER. All very well, Mr. Karslake, but I must know if I'm to give her—

JOHN. (*Turning over the leaves of the telephone book in hot haste.*) What's Phillimore's number?

FIDDLER. If you've no objections, I think I'll give her a—

JOHN. (*As before.*) L—M—N—O—P—It's too late! She's married by this! Married!—and—my God—I—I am the cause. Phillimore—

FIDDLER. I'll give her—

JOHN. Give her wheatina!—give her grape nuts—give her away! (FIDDLER *goes up.*) Only be quiet! Phillimore! (*Enter* SIR WILFRID, *back.*)

SIR WILFRID. Hello! We'd almost given you up!

JOHN. (*Still in his agitation unable to find Phillimore's number.*) Just a moment! I'm trying to get Phillimore on the phone to—to tell Mrs. Karslake—

SIR WILFRID. No good, my boy—she's on her way here! (JOHN *drops book and looks up dumbfounded.*) The Reverend Matthew was here, y' see—and he said—

JOHN. (*Rises; turns.*) Mrs. Karslake is coming here? (SIR WILFRID *nods.*) To this house? Here?

SIR WILFRID. That's right.

JOHN. Coming here? You're sure? (SIR WILFRID *nods assent.*) Fiddler (*Crosses* R., *to* FIDDLER. FIDDLER *comes* C.) I want you to stay here, and if Mrs. Karslake comes, don't fail to let me know! Now then, for Heaven's sake, what did Matthew say to you!

SIR WILFRID. Come along in and I'll tell you.

JOHN. On your life now, Fiddler, don't fail to let me— (*Exeunt* JOHN *and* SIR WILFRID.)

VIDA. (*Voice off.*) Ah, here you are!

FIDDLER. Phew! (*A moment's pause, and* CYNTHIA *enters. She comes in very quietly, almost shyly, and as if she were uncertain of her welcome.*)

CYNTHIA. Fiddler! Where is he? Has he come? Is he here? Has he gone?

FIDDLER. (*Rattled.*) Nobody's gone, ma'am, except the Reverend Matthew Phillimore.

CYNTHIA. Matthew? He's been here and gone? (FIDDLER *nods assent.*) You don't mean I'm too late? He's married them already?

FIDDLER. Nogam says he married them!

CYNTHIA. He's married them! Married! Married before I could get here! (*Sits in armchair.*) Married in less time than it takes to pray for rain! Oh, well, the church—the church is a regular quick marriage counter. (*Voices of* VIDA *and* JOHN *heard off in light-hearted laughter.*) Oh!

FIDDLER. I'll tell Mr. Karslake—

CYNTHIA. (*Rising and going to the door through which* JOHN *left the stage; she turns the key in the lock and takes it out.*) No—I wouldn't see him for the world! (*She comes down with key to the work-table.*) If I'm too late, I'm too late! and that's the end of it! (*She lays key on table* L.; *remains standing near it.*) I've come, and now I'll go! (*Long pause.* CYNTHIA *looks about the room; changes her tone.*) Well, Fiddler, it's all a good deal as it used to be in my day.

FIDDLER. No, ma'am—everything changed, even the horses.

CYNTHIA. (*Same business; absent-mindedly.*) Horses—how are the horses? (*Throughout this scene she gives the idea that she is saying good-bye to her life with* JOHN.)

FIDDLER. (R. C.) Ah, when husband and wife splits, ma'am, it's the horses that suffer. Oh, yes, ma'am, we're all changed since you give us the go-by,—even the guv'nor.

CYNTHIA. (L. C.) How's he changed?

FIDDLER. Lost his sharp for horses, and ladies, ma'am —gives 'em both the boiled eye.

CYNTHIA. (L. C., *down.*) I can't say I see any change; there's my portrait—I suppose he sits and pulls faces at me.

FIDDLER. Yes, ma'am, I think I'd better tell him of your bein' here.

CYNTHIA. (*Gently but decidedly.*) No, Fiddler, no! (*She again looks about her.*) The room's in a terrible state of disorder. However, your new mistress will attend to that. (*Pause.*) Why, that's not her hat!

FIDDLER. Yours, ma'am.

CYNTHIA. Mine? (*She goes to the table to look at it.*) Is that my work-basket? (*Pause.*) My gloves? (FIDDLER *assents.*) And I suppose— (*She hurriedly goes to the writing-table.*) My—yes, there it is: my wedding ring!—just where I dropped it! Oh, oh, oh, he keeps it like this—hat, gloves, basket and ring, everything just as it was that crazy, mad day when I— (*Glances at* FIDDLER *and breaks off.*) But for Heaven's sake, Fiddler, set that chair on its feet!

FIDDLER. Against orders, ma'am.

CYNTHIA. Against orders?

FIDDLER. You kicked it over, ma'am, the day you left us.

CYNTHIA. No wonder he hates me with the chair in that state! He nurses his wrath to keep it warm. So, after all, Fiddler, everything *is* changed, and that chair is the proof of it. I suppose Cynthia K is the only thing in the world that cares a whinney whether I'm alive or dead. (*She breaks down and sobs.*) How is she, Fiddler?

FIDDLER. Off her oats, ma'am, this evening.

CYNTHIA. Off her oats! Well, she loves me, so I suppose she will die, or change, or—or something. Oh, she'll die, there's no doubt about that—she'll die. (FIDDLER, *who has been watching his chance, takes the key off the table while she is sobbing, tiptoes up the stage, unlocks the door and goes out. After he has done so,* CYNTHIA *rises and dries her eyes.*) There—I'm a fool—I must go —before—before—he— (*As she speaks her last word* JOHN *comes on.*)

JOHN. Mrs. Karslake!

CYNTHIA. (*Confused.*) I—I—I just heard Cynthia K was ill— (JOHN *assents.* CYNTHIA *tries to put on a cheerful and indifferent manner.*) I—I—ran round—I —and—and— (*Pauses, turns, comes down.*) Well, I understand it's all over.

JOHN. (*Cheerfully.*) Yes, it's all over.

CYNTHIA. How is the bride?

JOHN. Oh, she's a wonder.

CYNTHIA. Indeed! Did she paw the ground like the war horse in the Bible? I'm sure when Vida sees a wedding ring she smells the battle afar off. As for you, my dear Karslake, I should have thought once bitten, twice shy! But, you know best. (*Enter* VIDA, *back* L.)

VIDA. Oh, Cynthia, I've just been through it again, and I feel as if I were eighteen. There's no use talking about it, my dear, with a woman it's never the second time! And how nice you were, Jack,—he never even laughed at us! (*Enter* SIR WILFRID, *with hat and cane.* VIDA *kisses* JOHN.) That's the wages of virtue!

SIR WILFRID. (*In time to see her kiss* JOHN.) I say, is it the custom? Every time she does that, my boy, you owe me a thousand pounds. (*Sees* CYNTHIA, *who comes down above chair; he looks at her and* JOHN *in turn.*) Mrs. Karslake. (*To* JOHN.) And then you say it's not an extraordinary country. (CYNTHIA *is more and more puzzled.*)

VIDA. (*To* JOHN.) See you next Derby, Jack! (*Crosses to door* R. *To* SIR WILFRID.) Come along, Wilfrid! We really ought to be going. (*To* CYNTHIA.) I hope, dear, you haven't married him! Phillimore's a tomb! Good-bye, Cynthia—I'm so happy! (*As she goes.*) Just think of the silly people, dear, that only have this sensation once in a lifetime! (*Exit* VIDA. JOHN *follows* VIDA *off.*)

SIR WILFRID. (*To* CYNTHIA.) Good-bye, Mrs. Karslake. And I say, ye know, if you have married that dull old Phillimore fellah, why when you've divorced him, come over and stay at Traynham! I mean, of course, ye know, bring your new husband. There'll be lots o' horses to show you, and a whole covey of jolly little Cates-Darbys. Mind you come! (*With real delicacy of feeling and forgetting his wife.*) Never liked a woman as much in my life as I did you!

VIDA. (*Outside; calling him.*) Wilfrid, dear!

SIR WILFRID. (*Loyal to the woman who has caught him.*) —except the one that's calling me! (*Reënter* JOHN. SIR WILFRID *nods to him and goes off.* JOHN *shuts door and crosses* L. *A pause.*)

CYNTHIA. So you're not married?

JOHN. No. But I know that you imagined I was. (*Pause.*)

CYNTHIA. I suppose you think a woman has no right to divorce a man—and still continue to feel a keen interest in his affairs?

JOHN. Well, I'm not so sure about that, but I don't quite see how—

CYNTHIA. A woman can be divorced—and—still— (JOHN *assents; she hides her embarrassment.*) Well, my dear Karslake, you've a long life before you, in which to learn how such a state of mind is possible! So I won't stop to explain. Will you be kind enough to get me a cab? (*She moves to the door.*)

JOHN. Certainly. I was going to say I am not surprised at your feeling an interest in me. I'm only astonished that, having actually married Phillimore, you come here—

CYNTHIA. (*Indignantly.*) I'm not married to him! (*A pause.*)

JOHN. I left you on the brink—made me feel a little uncertain.

CYNTHIA. (*In a matter of course tone.*) I changed my mind—that's all.

JOHN. (*Taking his tone from her.*) Of course. (*A pause.*) Are you going to marry him?

CYNTHIA. I don't know.

JOHN. Does he know you—

CYNTHIA. I told him I was coming here.

JOHN. Oh! He'll turn up here, then—eh? (CYNTHIA *is silent.*) And you'll go back with him, I suppose?

CYNTHIA. (*Talking at random.*) Oh—yes—I suppose so. I—I haven't thought much about it.

JOHN. (*Changes his tone.*) Well, sit down; do. Till he comes—talk it over. (*He places the armchair more comfortably for her.*) This is a more comfortable chair!

CYNTHIA. (*Shamefacedly.*) You never liked me to sit in that one!

JOHN. Oh, well—it's different now. (CYNTHIA *crosses and sits down* R., *near the upset chair. Long pause.* JOHN *crosses.*) You don't mind if I smoke?

CYNTHIA. (*Shakes her head.*) No.

JOHN. (*Business with pipe. Sits on arm of chair right of table* L.) Of course, if you find my presence painful, I'll—skiddoo. (*He indicates* L. CYNTHIA *shakes her head.* JOHN *smokes pipe and remains seated.*)

CYNTHIA. (*Suddenly and quickly.*) It's just simply a fact, Karslake, and that's all there is to it—if a woman has once been married—that is, the first man she marries—then—she may quarrel, she may hate him—she may despise him—but she'll always be jealous of him with other women. Always! (JOHN *takes this as if he were simply glad to have the information.*)

JOHN. Oh—Hm! ah—yes—yes. (*A pause.*)

CYNTHIA. You probably felt jealous of Phillimore.

JOHN. (*Reasonably, sweetly, and in doubt.*) N-o! I felt simply: Let him take his medicine. (*Apologetically.*)

CYNTHIA. Oh!

JOHN. I beg your pardon—I meant—

CYNTHIA. You meant what you said!

JOHN. (*Comes a step to her.*) Mrs. Karslake, I apologize—I won't do it again. But it's too late for you to be out alone—Philip will be here in a moment—and of course, then—

CYNTHIA. It isn't what you *say*—it's—it's—it's everything. It's the entire situation. Suppose by any chance I don't marry Phillimore! And suppose I were seen at two or three in the morning leaving my former husband's house! It's all wrong. I have no business to be here! I'm going! You're perfectly horrid to me, you know—and—the whole place—it's so familiar, and so—so associated with—with—

JOHN. Discord and misery—I know—

CYNTHIA. Not at all with discord and misery! With harmony and happiness—with—with first love, and infinite hope—and—and—Jack Karslake,—if you don't set that chair on its legs, I think I'll explode. (JOHN *crosses rapidly, sets chair on its legs. Change of tone.*)

JOHN. (*While setting chair on its legs,* R.) There! I beg your pardon.

CYNTHIA. (*Nervously.*) I believe I hear Philip. (*Rises.*)

JOHN. (*Goes up to window.*) N-o! That's the policeman trying the front door! And now, see here, Mrs. Karslake,—you're only here for a short minute, because you can't help yourself, but I want you to understand that I'm not trying to be disagreeable—I don't want to revive all the old unhappy—

CYNTHIA. Very well, if you don't—give me my hat. (JOHN *does so.*) And my sewing! And my gloves, please! (*She indicates the several articles which lie on the small table.*) Thanks! (CYNTHIA *throws the lot into the fireplace,* L., *and returns to the place she has left near table.*) There! I feel better! And now—all I ask is—

JOHN. (*Laughs.*) My stars, what a pleasure it is!

CYNTHIA. What is?

JOHN. Seeing you in a whirlwind!

CYNTHIA. (*Wounded by his seeming indifference.*) Oh!

JOHN. No, but I mean, a real pleasure! Why not? Time's passed since you and I were together—and—eh—

CYNTHIA. And you've forgotten what a vile temper I had!

JOHN. (*Reflectively.*) Well, you did kick the stuffing out of the matrimonial buggy—

CYNTHIA. (*Pointedly but with good temper.*) It wasn't a buggy; it was a break cart— (*She stands back of the armchair.*) It's all very well to blame me! But when you married me, I'd never had a bit in my mouth!

JOHN. Well, I guess I had a pretty hard hand. Do you remember the time you threw both your slippers out of the window?

CYNTHIA. Yes, and do you remember the time you took my fan from me by force?

JOHN. After you slapped my face with it!

CYNTHIA. Oh, oh! I hardly touched your face! And do you remember the day you held my wrists?

JOHN. You were going to bite me!

CYNTHIA. Jack! I never! I showed my teeth at you! And I said I would bite you!

JOHN. Cynthia, I never knew you to break your word! (*He laughs. Casually.*) And anyhow—they were awfully pretty teeth! (CYNTHIA, *though bolt upright, has ceased to seem pained.*) And I say—do you remember, Cyn— (*Leans over the armchair to talk to her.*)

CYNTHIA. (*After a pause.*) You oughtn't to call me "Cyn"—its not nice of you. It's sort of cruel. I'm not—Cyn to you now.

JOHN. Awfully sorry; didn't mean to be beastly, Cyn. (CYNTHIA *turns quickly.* JOHN *stamps his foot.*) Cynthia! Sorry. I'll make it a commandment; thou shalt not Cyn!! (CYNTHIA *laughs and wipes her eyes.*)

CYNTHIA. How can you, Jack? How can you?

JOHN. Well, hang it, my dear child, I—I'm sorry, but you know I always got foolish with you. Your laugh'd make a horse laugh. Why, don't you remember that morning in the park before breakfast—when you laughed so hard your horse ran away with you!

CYNTHIA. I do, I do! (*Both laugh. The door opens,* R. NOGAM *enters.*) But what was it started me laughing? (*Laughs. Sits. Laughs again.*) That morning. Wasn't it somebody we met? (*Laughs.*) Wasn't it a man on a horse? (*Laughs.*)

JOHN. (*Laughing too.*) Of course! You didn't know him in those days! But I did! And he looked a sight in the saddle! (NOGAM, *trying to catch their attention, comes down* R. *corner, right of table* R.)

CYNTHIA. Who was it?

JOHN. Phillimore!

CYNTHIA. He's no laughing matter now. (*Sees* NOGAM R.) Jack, he's here!

JOHN. Eh? Oh, Nogam?

NOGAM. Mr. Phillimore, sir—

JOHN. In the house?

NOGAM. On the street in a hansom, sir—and he requests Mrs. Karslake—

JOHN. That'll do, Nogam. (*Exit* NOGAM, R. *Pause.* JOHN *from near the window.* CYNTHIA *faces audience.*)

Well, Cynthia? (*He speaks almost gravely and with finality.*)

CYNTHIA. (*Trembling.*) Well?

JOHN. It's the hour of decision, are you going to marry him? (*Pause.*) Speak up!

CYNTHIA. Jack,—I—I—

JOHN. There he is—you can join him. (*He points to the street.*)

CYNTHIA. Join Phillimore—and go home—with him—to his house, and Miss Heneage and—

JOHN. The door's open. (*He points to the door.*)

CYNTHIA. No, no! It's mean of you to suggest it!

JOHN. You won't marry—

CYNTHIA. Phillimore—no; never. (*Runs to window.*) No; never, never, Jack.

JOHN. (*Goes up. He calls out of window, having opened it.*) It's all right, Judge. You needn't wait. (*Pause.* JOHN *comes down. Tableau.* JOHN *bursts into laughter.* CYNTHIA *looks dazed. He closes door.*)

CYNTHIA. Jack! (JOHN *laughs.*) Yes, but I'm here, Jack.

JOHN. Why not?

CYNTHIA. You'll have to take me round to the Holland House!

JOHN. Of course, I will! But, I say, Cynthia, there's no hurry.

CYNTHIA. Why, I—I—can't stay here.

JOHN. No, of course you can't stay here. But you can have a bite, though. (CYNTHIA *shakes her head.* JOHN *places the small chair which was upset, next to table* R. *Armchair above* R. C.) Oh, I insist. Just look at yourself—you're as pale as a sheet and—here, here. Sit right down. I insist! By George, you must do it! (CYNTHIA *crosses to chair beside table* R., *left of it, and sits.*)

CYNTHIA. (*Faintly.*) I *am* hungry.

JOHN. Just wait a moment. (JOHN *exits* L., *upper door, leaving it open.*)

CYNTHIA. I don't want more than a nibble! (*Pause.*) I am sorry to give you so much trouble.

JOHN. No trouble at all. (*He can be heard off* L., *busied with glasses and a tray.*) A hansom of course, to take you round to your hotel? (*Speaks as he comes down* R.)

CYNTHIA. (*To herself.*) I wonder how I ever dreamed I could marry that man.

JOHN. (*Above table by this time.*) Can't imagine! There!

CYNTHIA. I am hungry. Don't forget the hansom. (*She eats; he waits on her, setting this and that before her.*)

JOHN. (*Goes to door* R., *up; opens it and speaks off.*) Nogam, a hansom at once.

NOGAM. (*Off stage.*) Yes, sir.

JOHN. (*Back to above table; from here on he shows his feelings for her.*) How does it go?

CYNTHIA. (*Faintly.*) It goes all right. Thanks! (*Hardly eating at all.*)

JOHN. You always used to like anchovy. (CYNTHIA *nods and eats.*) Claret? (CYNTHIA *shakes her head.*) Oh, but you must!

CYNTHIA. (*Tremulously.*) Ever so little. (*He fills her glass and then sits.*) Thanks! (*He pours out a glass for himself.*)

JOHN. Here's to old times! (*Raising glass.*)

CYNTHIA. (*Very tremulous.*) Please not!

JOHN. Well, here's to your next husband.

CYNTHIA. (*Very tenderly.*) Don't!

JOHN. Oh, well, then, what shall the toast be?

CYNTHIA. I'll tell you— (*Pause.*) you can drink to the relation I am to you!

JOHN. (*Laughing.*) Well—what relation are you?

CYNTHIA. I'm your first wife once removed!

JOHN. (*Laughs; drinks.*) I say, you're feeling better.

CYNTHIA. Lots.

JOHN. (*Reminiscent.*) It's a good deal like those mornings after the races—isn't it?

CYNTHIA. (*Nods.*) Yes. Is that the hansom? (*Half rises.*)

JOHN. (*Going up to the window.*) No.

CYNTHIA. (*Sits again.*) What is that sound?

JOHN. Don't you remember?

CYNTHIA. No.

JOHN. That's the rumbling of the early milk wagons.

CYNTHIA. Oh, Jack.

JOHN. Do you recognize it now?

CYNTHIA. Do I? We used to hear that—just at the hour, didn't we—when we came back from awfully jolly late suppers and things!

JOHN. H'm!

CYNTHIA. It must be fearfully late. I must go. (*Rises, crosses to* L. *chair, where she has left cloak. She sees that* JOHN *will not help her and puts it on herself.*)

JOHN. Oh, don't go—why go?

CYNTHIA. (*Embarrassed and agitated.*) All good things come to an end, you know.

JOHN. They don't need to.

CYNTHIA. Oh, you don't mean that! And, you know, Jack, if I were caught—seen at this hour, leaving this house, you know—it's the most scandalous thing any one ever did my being here at all. (*Crosses to* R. C.) Good-bye, Jack! (*Pause; almost in tears.*) I'd like to say, I—I—I—well, I shan't be bitter about you hereafter, and— (*Pause.*) Thank you awfully, old man, for the fodder and all that! (*Turns to go out* R. *upper.*)

JOHN. Mrs. Karslake—wait—

CYNTHIA. (*Stopping to hear.*) Well?

JOHN. (*Serious.*) I've rather an ugly bit of news for you.

CYNTHIA. Yes?

JOHN. I don't believe you know that I have been testing the validity of the decree of divorce which you procured.

CYNTHIA. Oh, have you?

JOHN. Yes; you know I felt pretty warmly about it.

CYNTHIA. Well?

JOHN. Well, I've been successful. (*Pause.*) The decree's been declared invalid. Understand?

CYNTHIA. (*Looks at him a moment; then speaks.*) Not—precisely.

JOHN. (*Pause.*) I'm awfully sorry—I'm awfully sorry, Cynthia, but, you're my wife still. (*Pause.*)

CYNTHIA. (*With rapture.*) Honor bright? (*She sinks into the armchair.*)

JOHN. (*Nods. Half laughingly.*) Crazy country, isn't it?

CYNTHIA. (*Nods. Pause.*) Well, Jack—what's to be done?

JOHN. (*Gently.*) Whatever you say. (*Moves* C.)

NOGAM. (*Quietly enters door* R.) Hansom, sir. (*Exits;* CYNTHIA *rises.*)

JOHN. Why don't you finish your supper? (CYNTHIA *hesitates.*)

CYNTHIA. The—the—hansom—

JOHN. Why go to the Holland? After all—you know, Cyn, you're at home here.

CYNTHIA. No, Jack, I'm not—I'm not at home here—unless—unless—

JOHN. Out with it!

CYNTHIA. (*Bursting into tears.*) Unless I—unless I'm at home in your heart, Jack!

JOHN. What do you think?

ACT IV THE NEW YORK IDEA 125

CYNTHIA. I don't believe you want me to stay.

JOHN. Don't you?

CYNTHIA. No, no, you hate me still. You never can forgive me. I know you can't. For I can never forgive myself. Never, Jack, never, never! (*She sobs and he takes her in his arms.*)

JOHN. (*Very tenderly.*) Cyn! I love you! (*Strongly.*) And you've got to stay! And hereafter you can chuck chairs around till all's blue! Not a word now. (*He draws her gently to a chair.*)

CYNTHIA. (*Wiping her tears.*) Oh, Jack! Jack!

JOHN. I'm as hungry as a shark. We'll nibble together.

CYNTHIA. Well, all I can say is, I feel that of all the improprieties I ever committed this—this—

JOHN. This takes the claret, eh? Oh, Lord, how happy I am!

CYNTHIA. Now don't say that! You'll make me cry more. (*She wipes her eyes.* JOHN *takes out wedding ring from his pocket; he lifts a wine glass, drops the ring into it and offers her the glass.*)

JOHN. Cynthia!

CYNTHIA. (*Looking at it and wiping her eyes.*) What is it?

JOHN. Benedictine!

CYNTHIA. Why, you know I never take it.

JOHN. Take this one for my sake.

CYNTHIA. That's not benedictine. (*With gentle curiosity.*) What is it?

JOHN. (*He slides the ring out of the glass and puts his arm about* CYNTHIA. *He slips the ring on to her finger and, as he kisses her hand, says.*) Your wedding ring!

CURTAIN

OTHER TITLES AVAILABLE FROM BAKER'S PLAYS

HOW THE OTHER HALF LOVES

Alan Ayckbourn

Farce / 3m, 3f / interior

There are three couples in this play; the men all work for the same firm. One of the younger men is having an affair with the wife of the oldest. When each returns home suspiciously late one night, they invent a story about having to smooth domestic troubles for the third couple.

OTHER TITLES AVAILABLE FROM BAKER'S PLAYS

KISS ME QUICK, I'M DOUBLE PARKED

John Kirkpatrick

Farce / 5m, 7f / interior

Things were hectic in the office of Alex, a young dentist. On his way to get married, his bride was marooned on the twenty-second floor by an elevator strike, and his secretary was not sympathetic. When the garbage collectors tried to cross the picket lines, there were demonstrations by the parents and teachers from the public school on the corner. When you add to this the Con Edison people digging up the sidewalk, a masked bandit and a broken gas main which threatens to blow up the building, is it any wonder that Alex almost eloped with the wrong woman?

OTHER TITLES AVAILABLE FROM BAKER'S PLAYS

EVERYBODY'S CRAZY

Jay Tobias

Farce / 8m, 7f / interior

Three young college men take on more than they can handle when they buy a summer hotel. Business is bad — so very bad that it becomes necessary to give the hotel a reputation as a haven for ghosts, and the secret hiding place of an old miser's hoard of gold. That brings in the guests — though perhaps not the kind the young men are looking for: an elderly spiritualist, a sleep-walking Romeo and his hypochondriac wife, and a farmer prone to nightmares. One of the boys impersonates a doctor and treats the guests for all sorts of imagined ailments, another assumes a feminine disguise and sets many a masculine heart beating!

OTHER TITLES AVAILABLE FROM BAKER'S PLAYS

THE COOLEY GIRLS

Brad Stephens

Dramatic Comedy / 1m, 5f

Three sisters, Rose, Brenda and Harriet Cooley, have been separated since childhood. Now forty years later, one of the sisters, Rose, decides to find her lost siblings and reunite the 'girls'. All of them have secrets to hide, but it is curiosity that finally brings them together for their unexpected reunion. Only when Harriet is forced to admit her most damning secret does this hard-bitten and humorous play resolve once and for all the bond each shares with the other. Perfect for community stages.

OTHER TITLES AVAILABLE FROM BAKER'S PLAYS

SEE YOU IN BELLS

Edie Claire

Comedy / 6m, 6f, 2 teen girls, 1 teen boy, and a good-natured minister / A church sanctuary

The mother of the bride has every reason to panic. Three generations of Bower family weddings—three inexplicable disasters. Now, with the church building falling down, half the wedding party AWOL, and the bride's sisters still fighting over what happened at the last family wedding, daughter Jenna's nuptials seem hopelessly doomed. But peacemaking brother Brian is determined to end the sisters' feud—and the family curse. All he needs is to stage a rip-roaring intervention…and pray it turns divine!

BAKERSPLAYS.COM

OTHER TITLES AVAILABLE FROM BAKER'S PLAYS

KEEPSAKES

Pat Cook

Drama / 4m, 6f / Interior

Ever look at a family portrait and wonder what those people, posed and smiling, are really like? This family portrait shows you the inner workings of the Rogers family – how they deal with everyday things, how they deal with both happy and sad events which effect each and every one of them. These funny, poignant and all-too-human characters go through life the best way they know how.

Austin does his best to keep the house running smoothly, unless he has to take Pawpaw's trunk out of the basement. Mary Jo is outwardly pleased when son Mitchell gets engaged to Tish but explains "They're too young!" Her sister, Brenda, helps out by saying "Not any younger than you were when you got married." Brenda's husband, Dale, has his own advice for young Mitchell – "Marriage consists in large part of just giving up!" And Pawpaw keeps hearing voices and seeing people who aren't there.

The very fabric of the family unit meets its ultimate challenge when Brenda and Dale have to move in with them. Daughter Jan has to put up with a whiney dog, Mitchell and Tish can't seem to find time to talk about their upcoming marriage and everyone is bunking up with everyone else, leaving the men to sleep on the couch – any of this sound familiar? Brought to you by the same author of *Good Help is So Hard to Murder.*

BAKERSPLAYS.COM

www.ingramcontent.com/pod-product-compliance
Lightning Source LLC
Chambersburg PA
CBHW072338300426
44109CB00042B/1696